CARVE

Carve: How to Steward and Sustain a Move of God

ISBN: 978-1-955546-00-3

A Publication of Tall Pine Books
| tallpinebooks.com

*Published in the United States of America

CARVE

HOW TO STEWARD AND SUSTAIN A MOVE OF GOD.

DARREN STOTT

"Many are sensing now the greatest Awakening in human history. Fresh hope and expectation are beginning to rise around the world as we gain a glimpse of Heaven's intention for the hour, we're living in. The book you hold in your hands contains vital wisdom required for all that's ahead. As Darren Stott states, 'The question isn't is God willing but rather are we ready!' This powerful book is right on time, written by a true friend of Jesus. It ignites faith and provides vision and equipping that will cause us to thrive as we understand more clearly than ever God's intention for our lives."

—LIZ WRIGHT
International Best-Selling Author, *Reflecting God*
Host of *Podcast Show, Live Your Best Life with Liz Wright*
available on the Charisma platform

"Darren Stott is a personal friend and comrade in the faith. He presents cutting-edge truth with a creative and often humorous flare. His latest book will bless you."

—PATRICIA KING
Author, Minister, Media Host

"I am so thankful for this timely book! In these days of great challenge and turmoil, God's Spirit is releasing Revival Glory to those who are willing to dig deeper and find their place in Him. Darren shows us how to carve a realm in the Spirit and occupy it for the glory of God! The revelation in this book has been proven through Darren's life and ministry experiences, and it will work in your life too! Read this book, follow the divine instructions and see the wonderful things that God will do!"

— JOSHUA MILLS
Author, Minister, Media Host
bestselling author of "*Power Portals*"
Founder, *International Glory Ministries*

"Sometimes God keeps a next-level leader hidden for decades before He takes the lid off and joyfully exclaims, "Tada!" King Jesus is unveiling His strategy for revival through the anointed message of my friend Darrin Stott. He's serious about the Kingdom coming without taking himself very seriously. I find Darrin refreshing and much needed in this age of a whole new wineskin."

—TROY BREWER
Founder, Senior Pastor, *Open Door Church*

"I love Darren Stott! He is funny, inspirational, and wise. A rare package indeed! His church SRC is the real thing, creating a culture where Jesus feels at home, where miracles happen, people are healed, and community flourishes. Darren is also a recognized voice outside the church, helping shape the Seattle region and beyond. Read this book. Enjoy it. Let it inspire you to live a bigger wilder life. The best is yet to come!"

—JUSTIN ABRAHAM
Company of Burning Hearts

"If revival is a big, beautiful, juicy steak, then Carves the utensil to eat that steak. So, steak isn't your thing? This book will make you crave more of God regardless, and it offers personal and corporate gems to sustaining your passion."

—STEVE SWANSON
Friends of the Bridegroom Worship Ministries

"I would like to highly recommend my good friend Darren Stott's new book, *Carve: How to Steward and Sustain a Move of God*. In this book, you will learn how to live a revival lifestyle from one of the best stewards of revival I know. Darren not only carries a ton of revelation concerning sustaining a move of God, but he has actually hosted one. Many write out of a place of theory. Still, Darren is a revival practitioner and has practical experience in hosting hundreds of nights of protracted meetings, making him an expert on this subject."

—JERAME NELSON
Founder, Elisha Revolution
Author, *Portals of Revelation, Burning Ones,*
and *Living Under an Open Heaven*

"The best books are written by authors who walk the walk and talk the talk. Darren is one of those authors. He is a third-generation revivalist who understands that we have been promised the Manifest Presence of God. Acts 2:17 makes that clear, and God says in Ezekiel 39:29 that He will not hide his face from us anymore.

In his book *Carve*, Darren slices up some good meat for us to chew on, including humor to help us swallow the portions to learn to steward and maintain a move of God. Every testimony of a revival or move of God includes stories about the manifest presence of God. I love the statement in his book, *"What if, at every gathering, there was a manifestation of Jesus? We would have to start selling tickets."* This manifest presence makes everyone with a spirit, whether saved or unsaved conscious of God. Great Awakening's do that, and Darren helps us as leaders to have an expectation for it. God once told a friend of mine who was struggling to receive from the Lord that, "It isn't disbelief it's your expectation."

Carve reminds us of the importance of expectation and gives us the tools to create and sustain atmospheres where God show up. This book is a must-read for every leader and individual who has a heart that is hungry for Him. We must have His manifest presence in our midst because religion will not satisfy any soul."

—GREG DALEY
President, *International Fellowship of Ministries*,
Founder, *Fire of His Love Ministries*

"Reading *Carve* by Darren Stott was like experiencing a face-melting guitar solo. I began to vibrate, and my countenance began to glow like Moses and I even levitated a little as I was moved by the words on each page. Carve is a revival recipe that I know will shift your community into the "more" of God. I highly recommend this book!"

—ALEX PARKINSON
Author, *Spirit Without Measure*
Zionco.Org

"Hilarious heavy revy at the speed of light. We encourage everyone to read *Carve* by Darren Stott. It is the perfect recipe of humor, practicality, relatability, all while giving keys to cultivating and sustaining revival.

This isn't just a book to read, but an invitation to bring revival and transformation everywhere you go."

—AARON AND BETH PACKARD
Founder, *Gathering Revival Center*

"As you read the following pages, you will find deep hunger for Awakening ignited in your heart! Wisdom is carried on the wings of Darren's joy, humor, and testimony. He carries a heart for the presence of God like few I've known. His character is matched with his undying commitment to see the Kingdom of God established on earth as it is in Heaven. The book you are holding is written by a dread champion. You will find joy and fire here. Let the carving begin!"

—ELISABETH COOPER
Elisabeth Cooper Ministries

"Darren Stott brilliantly and passionately brings to light a supernatural lifestyle that will equip you to "Carve" out a never-ending revival of Heaven on Earth."

—MICHAEL DANFORTH
Mountain Top International and *Danforth Ministries*

"If you are looking for ways to steward revival in your church and city, I highly recommend this book. Darren has not only been stewarding revival in his church, but he has also been living out revival in his everyday life. *Carve* is the book that every pastor needs to have in their library to see revival become a lifestyle and not a season in their church."

—JOSH SCHEIDLER
Lead Pastor, *Ignite Faith Church* Redmond OR.

"Pastor Darren Stott is a brilliant & prophetic voice for this generation. In this book, supernatural revival fire will capture you instantly. This Revelatory book will lead you to a greater expectation for "More of God"! Carve is a must-read for all those that are seekers of the unseen Realms of God!"

—JONATHAN CORONADO
The Journey Church, Yakima WA

"Darren Stott's latest book shows you the pathways into the presence and move of God. Here are revelations that get results. Darren shares teachings you can trust. Prepare to see Jesus move like never before!!!!"

—PASTOR TONY KEMP
President, *Acts Group*
Vice President, *It's Supernatural and Supernatural Network*

"It's a glorious and beautiful thing to see the Lord move in our midst. Yet we need to realize that God wants to do way more than simply move. He wants to inhabit, occupy and transform. In his new book, CARVE, Darren Stott takes us beyond all the good teaching we've had on how to see a move of God stirred and birthed. He shares from experience how we can actually see a move sustained so that it brings permanent transformation to our churches, nations, lives, families and more. Needed, important and AWESOME!"

—ROBERT HOTCHKIN
Men on the Frontlines / Robert Hotchkin Ministries
roberthotchkin.com

"Many Christians, including leaders, think that some superstar can instigate a good glory meeting while jamming to some hot worship, believing this will bring the glory down and initiate revival. Darren Stott has experienced revival and knows what it takes. A revival doesn't just happen. It takes discipline, hard work, and heaps of grace, as Darren wrote. From beginning to end, Darren's latest book, *Carve*, provides the keys to stewarding and sustaining a revival, including Expectation, Preparation, Communication, Collaboration, Celebration, and Evaluation.

Over the years, I have been in quite a few revivals close up, and I am profoundly impressed with Darren's creative humor and critical approach to revival, which is essential for these days. Do not delay. This book is needed now, as I encourage you to spread the word to others about this phenomenal book written in the right season."

—DON MILAM
Acquisitions Consultant, *Whitaker House Publishers*
Author, *The Ancient Language of Eden*

"What if a life of unending adventure, beauty, purity, and justice was not a myth? What if the church was more than just another boring weekly event? My good friend, Darren Stott, asks these questions in his latest book, Carve, and I promise you the answers are there. I am pretty sure that everyone craves a defining moment that would make their life meaningful. What you seek, you will find inside Darren's book.

When you open his book, get ready for a big bang moment that will awaken you and lead you to a world of kingdom reality. You will learn how to carve out a realm where a move of God can be sustained in your home, your business, and your church.

Darren introduces the importance of carving out six principles that will help you protect the anointing on your life and a move of the Spirit within this generation. The six principles are Expectation, Preparation, Communication, Collaboration, Celebration, Evaluation.

As Darren writes in his book, we have been deputized with the authority and ability to execute justice on the earth. It will be hard work. It will be painful, but together, we can create heavenly communities on planet earth."

—CHARLIE SHAMP
Co-founder, *Destiny Encounters International*
Author, *Transfigured*

This book is dedicated to Carmelo Domenic Licciardello.

As a child, you demonstrated to me what it meant to be an out-of-the-box minister. Whether you were breakdancing, preaching, or dressing up like a cowboy and shooting Satan, you masterfully coupled storytelling with the power of the Holy Spirit.

The world will miss you greatly, and you can be well assured, you'll be one of the first guys I look up when I get to Heaven.

Carmen
01/19/1956 – 02/16/2021

CONTENTS

FOREWORD

"After these things I looked, and behold, a <u>door</u> standing open in heaven, and the first voice which I had heard, like the sound of a trumpet speaking with me, said, "<u>Come up here, and I will show you</u> what must take place after these things."
—Revelation 4:1, NASB

'Revivals are not unicorns. They are portals, and *they exist.*' These are the words of Pastor Darren Stott in *Carve,* his straight shooting, powerful, confrontation with the spiritual reality called 'revival.' He claims revival is a door between realms of the seen and unseen. A dimension of body and soul wholeness in "back to Eden realities of heaven on earth." Not just boisterous nightly events in a church building but rather a vibrant, mystical union with God and man that terraforms the earth. He speaks from experience.

Darren Stott is one of the most courageous men we know. We have watched him take on pandemic, politics, and protests, in the Presence and power of God. His creative genius and irrepressible joy made him the nightly news highlight and morning newspaper headliner. His honesty is disarming, his joy irresistible. He has harnessed the slew of gifting that has empowered him to thrive in any enterprise and poured himself into one mission: Christ in you manifest in pursuit of eternal destinies and reclaiming a world that groans under the weight of its own chaos. Revival not just for individuals, although individuals are the wineskins out of whom this wine is poured into our world, revival for families, whole communities, and if you will believe it, for your city, your nation—with you right in the middle of it.

The possibility of two existence continuums operating in a dance together wherein beauty leads, grace guides, joy holds us in the embrace and God directs our steps makes me recall a moment a few years back when Darren was riding along in the car with his then 5-year-old daughter who suddenly blurted out a 'poem' she composed on the spot. Sophie said,

> *"Playground is the Earth.*
> *Playground for Heaven— it's all white.*
> *It's cutted in half.*
> *Those halves come together, and they make a playground.*
> *Earth goes on the bottom,*
> *Heaven goes on the top.*
> *They are combined.*
> *But God controls one.*
> *Sin has control of the other.*
> *There is tape that sticks on to something until it gets moved.*
> *The tape is called The Standard.*
> *The Earth and Heaven get that special tape to stick together.*
> *If they lose that special tape, then they fall apart.*
> *Different countries have different heavens and different gods, and they should choose the right one.*
> *It hurts, people don't want to think, but it's the mind that has to choose.*
> *Let the mind choose.*
> *Let's pretend someone wanted to choose sin but they can't, do you know why?*
> *Because of The Standard.*

*When somebody prays and says that they choose God, God hears
them He puts a star on top of the heaven roof."*

In her words, revival just might be The Standard. And you
choosing to carve revival out of our world might just be the star
on heaven's roof.

The iconic figure of revival, Smith Wigglesworth, during the
dark days of World War II, had a vision for the greatest revival in
history. Evangelist Lester Sumrall tells the story of Wigglesworth
sharing that vision with him in 1939:

"... Shutting his eyes again, he said, 'I see the greatest revival
in the history of mankind coming to Planet earth, maybe as
never before. And I see every form of disease healed. I see
whole hospitals emptied with no one there. Even the doctors are running down the streets shouting.' Sumrall continues, "He told me that there would be untold numbers of
uncountable multitudes that would be saved. No man will
say 'so many, so many,' because nobody will be able to count
those who come to Jesus. No disease will be able to stand
before God's people... 'It will be a worldwide situation, not
local,' he said, 'a worldwide thrust of God's power and God's
anointing upon mankind.' And in the last decade or so, I
believe we have seen this revival begin to sweep the earth.
We have seen amazing moves of God in Africa... Recently, I
was in China and met with the underground church. I discovered a depth of prayer and integrity there that I have not
felt anywhere else in the world... So, I believe we are seeing
Wigglesworth's prophecy begin to be fulfilled. We are seeing
the first stages of it."

Carve unfolds six powerful keys for your best life intending
that we be fully untethered from what Stott calls the 'lousy barometer' of our soul that sulks in the corner not recognizing the
moment God who guides the universe has invaded our sphere.

Darren's invitation is to prophets, poets, creatives, seeker, novice, sage, and martyr, alike. Stott writes, "Since the fall of man, our sinister enemy has done his dastardly best to keep humanity from returning to the garden, where we enjoy the daily walks with God. ...Sin consciousness is like a cruel magician who tricks us into believing that our sin has zipped up the veil, like an old tent, closing the portal between us and God, therefore preventing our return to Eden....What if someone was knocking at your door, and when you opened the door, Jesus was staring you in the face, and then he said, "Come follow me."

This book is timely. Darren is with us in the room, in our ear, down to earth and otherworldly. While reading the first few chapters (it was well after midnight) two things occurred simultaneously outside my door—intense melodic birdsong and noisy abundant rainfall. I was immediately revisited by the hallmarks of those seasons supernatural visitation we have witnessed over forty-five years of global engagement. It seemed creation was underscoring the message coming to me in *Carve*. I was reminded that Charles Finney, in his testimonial of the "burnt through district" revivals that swept the Ohio Valley during the 19th century, tells of whole cities' which social order and economies surrendered to the intervention of God through spiritual visitation and renewal. Finney wrote, "Revival comes from heaven when heroic souls enter the conflict determined to win or die—or if need be—to win and die! The kingdom of heaven suffers violence and the violent take it by force." In *Carve*, Darren draws from a broad field of inquiry, study of scripture, the testament of men and women past and present who champion the faith realm, from his personal engagement in culture, family, and community, and his own unusual call to this higher way, to carve out six disciplines that are keys to crossing the Rubicon of the Spirit into revival realm.

Carve invites you to dive into scripture, the origins and language of revival and revival culture, and clear up the things that otherwise restrain personal encounter with Christ as an elusive, one time, or sporadic advent—and become, instead, the authentic relational state of being you were created for. With uncommon insight, Darren unwraps the strategic design behind celebration, collaboration with God, communication beyond one sided prayer where He hardly gets in a word edgewise, and elevation to a lifestyle through the revival portal. What if a life of *unending* adventure, beauty, purity, and justice is not a myth?

Revival doesn't just happen. It is contagious...let it catch you. It's time to *Carve*.

—BONNIE CHAVDA
All Nations Church
The Watch of the Lord
Charlotte/Ft. Mill, the Carolinas

INTRODUCTION

"Ladies and gentlemen, the Captain has turned on the fasten seat belt sign. We are now crossing a zone of turbulence. Please return your seats and keep your seat belts fastened. Thank you."

The 777-300ER began to shake as the pilot slowed the aircraft down to turbulence penetration speed, providing the least amount of stress to be put on the airplane. The turbulence itself, as bad as it was, was not what was shaking the young man in seat 22D.

In an attempt to hide my weeping, I pulled a blanket over my face. While tears poured down my cheeks, the glory of the Lord only intensified. It felt as though the Lord was waiting for a response, "What is your answer, my son?"

The trip to Indonesia was coming to an end; soon, the plane would land in Seattle. A collection of revival highlights that would climax into prophetic confrontations played through my imagination like an IMAX movie. Night after night, miracles, signs and wonders, salvations, would culminate into conversations between various pastors and myself.

The conversation was always the same.

"Where do you pastor?"

"I am not a pastor. I'm in business."

"Nope. You are a pastor."

I asked myself why I ever agree to follow in my dad's footsteps if that meant that I would have to experience the same heartbreak? There, in my brokenness, Father God leaned into the tension, "Darren, you don't trust me." At which point I responded, "You are right. I don't."

Air pockets didn't cause turbulence in the sky, (which by the way, don't exist). There is no such thing as airspace void of air where airplanes fly. Like no ocean is free of waves, no revival is free of fire. In the 1990's revival, the fire of God burned hot and bright to the point where I came to hate it. I believed that it was a revival that burned my family, my church, and my identity. When it was done burning, I felt like there was once a beautiful thick forest, but now there was just me, standing amongst charred stumps and smoldering smoke. I would fend for myself, protect myself, and trust no one, but did that mean not trusting God? I didn't particularly appreciate saying that I didn't trust God. Saying it just made me cry all the more.

How could I not trust God? What did that say about me? Was I somehow more trustworthy than God? Did I believe that I would make for a better shepherd than God himself? Did I think that I loved me more than He loved me? I knew better than that. During this period in my life, I certainly acted like an idiot, but that didn't make me a fool.

This moment on the plane wasn't ultimately about my call into ministry as much as it was about my total surrender.

Slowly, I pulled the blanket back down so I could read my Bible. It fell open to Isaiah 61.

The Spirit of the Lord God is upon me,
because the Lord has anointed me
to bring good news to the poor;
he has sent me to bind up the brokenhearted,

to proclaim liberty to the captives,
and the opening of the prison to those who are bound;
to proclaim the year of the Lord's favor,
and the day of vengeance of our God;
to comfort all who mourn;
to grant to those who mourn in Zion—
to give them a beautiful headdress instead of ashes,
the oil of gladness instead of mourning,
the garment of praise instead of a faint spirit;
that they may be called oaks of righteousness,
the planting of the Lord, that he may be glorified.
They shall build up the ancient ruins;
they shall raise up the former devastations;
they shall repair the ruined cities,
the devastations of many generations.

I knew this text was about Jesus, but I also felt that I had an essential role in this. The Father leaned in closer, His breath hot on my face as He said, "Reread it, but insert your name."

DARREN, the Spirit of the Lord God is upon you,
because the Lord has anointed you
to bring good news to the poor;
he has sent you to bind up the brokenhearted,
to proclaim liberty to the captives,
and the opening of the prison to those who are bound;
to proclaim the year of the Lord's favor,
and the day of vengeance of our God;
to comfort all who mourn;
to grant to those who mourn in Zion—
to give them a beautiful headdress instead of ashes,
the oil of gladness instead of mourning,
the garment of praise instead of a faint spirit;
that they may be called oaks of righteousness,
the planting of the Lord, that he may be glorified.

They shall build up the ancient ruins;
they shall raise up the former devastations;
they shall repair the ruined cities,
the devastations of many generations.

Years later, after my dad's passing, Andrea, Abigail, Peter, Sophia, and I sat at a Jakarta restaurant with Pastor Ginting and his beautiful family. I needed to see him. I needed to tell him that every part of his prophetic word for me had come true.

Twelve years prior, in a Pizza Hut in Jakarta, Pastor Ginting reached over the table, placed his hands upon my head, and prophesied over me. He spoke of my future, my wife, kids, ministry, and inheritance. He said, "Darren, you will come back to Indonesia, but next time, you will come without your father, and when you see me, you can call me papa."

On October 17th, 2016, Pastor Ginting laid his hands upon Andrea, my children, and myself. He blessed us with a Father's blessings, with an apostolic blessing, with the blessing of a revivalist. The presence of God's faithfulness was overwhelming.

Many different atmospheric conditions can cause turbulence, which in turn is rated from light to extreme intensity, how we respond while shaking can determine the trajectory of families, churches, cities, and nations.

As our country sits in the turbulence, a Church shakes with a blanket pulled over her face. The Father waits for the answer from His trembling bride. Will she trust God and embrace the fire and reproach associated with true revival, or will she choose to stay in control and manufacture Kingdom outcomes in the comfort of convenience and control?

I knew that attempting to remain the architect of my own life would only enable me to keep making selfish choices that eventually led to further brokenness. Despite my fear, I knew that trusting the Lord would ultimately lead to my security and safety.

As we began our descent back into Seattle, I responded to the Lord with, "Yes," and He responded to me with, "Do not fear; I will equip you with the wisdom that you will need to do what I have called you to do."

This is why I wrote this book. In the same way that the Lord has committed to prepare me to ride the waves of His spirit, I have made a similar commitment to equip the saints so that they can burn bright without burning out. Marriages, families, churches, schools, and regions do not have to suffer because men and women of God have not taken the time to carve out their boundaries, disciplines, and values.

My prayer is that this book would give you the faith to say "Yes" to God and that it would assist you as you begin carving out a realm of awakening within your own life. We will see His Kingdom come, and His will be done through a mature generation of sons and daughters who are walking in and releasing the manifest glory of God.

"Flight attendants, prepare for landing, please."

"Cabin crew, please take your seats for landing."

CHAPTER ONE

UNICORNS AND PORTALS

"As long as we are content to live without revival, we will."
—Leonard Ravenhill

NEAR-DEATH SIBERIAN RHINO ENCOUNTER

MARTY'S FACE WAS pale. While sitting on the curbside, his friends tried to calm him down by fanning his face and reminding him to breathe. It was too dark to see if his pants were wet. Still, everybody knew the smell of urine was not coming from his cherry slushy he obsessively slurped away despite finishing it about ten minutes prior. The paramedics finally arrived, like the X-Men, only disorganized and tardy.

"Good God," one of the paramedics said when he first saw Marty's pasty face. "The kid looks like he's seen a ghost."

Hours later, in the safety of a sterilized hospital room, Marty described a creature that would make Governor Cuomo speechless. Sitting up in his hospital bed and yanking the oxygen tubes from his nose, he shouted, "It... had... one... large, pointed, spiraling horn, protruding from its forehead!"

From the sounds of it, Peter Jenkin's kid was lucky to be alive. He just had a near-death encounter with the beast that Marty's eleventh-grade biology teacher, Mr. Depke, called "The Siberian Rhino." But Marty did not choose the title of Siberian Rhino to disclose the monster's identity; no, Marty chose the name given to the biblical creature that King David, Isaiah, and Job mentioned in the scriptures.

Licking his lips and stretching, he opened his jaws, and while attempting to speak through his uncomfortably dry cottonmouth, he said four words that cost everybody in the room at least one good night's rest.

"She... was... a... unicorn."

After having his stomach pumped, the toxicology results confirmed his friend's testimony. At approximately 7:15 pm, the report revealed that Marty Jenkins purchased a large cup of "cherry Kool-Aid" from a girl he said looked like an enchanting mermaid walking in the dimly lit parking lot of the Portland City Fair. Being quite taken with the girl's appearance, Marty agreed to pay forty-five dollars for a drink that contained more LSD than it did cherries. At 11:00 pm, Marty's friends finally located him. They were thrilled to discover that he was not kidnapped, as they supposed, but rather an alluring unicorn invited him to cross into another world that he called the Enchanted Autonomous Zone or EAZ. It turns out that EAZ, the world of fairy horses, did not exist. After hours of thumping, reality began to descend like a fog. The delight morphed into disappointment when Marty discovered he had trapped himself for almost four hours in the trunk of his dad's borrowed 1954 Buick Skylark.

Plastered on their front page, the Oregonian thoroughly covered the story, generously sharing Marty's account of what they titled, *An Encounter with a Unicorn*. Every time Marty glanced at the newspaper, tucked under his pillow, his cheeks would blush with the same reddish hue as his hallucinogenic drink. The hardest part for Marty to grasp wasn't that he had so publicly embarrassed himself, but rather the betrayal in finding out that the girl who looked like a mermaid was not actually named Starbright; that was her drug-dealing alias. Her real name was Karen Brody. Karen was an unemployed veterinarian who had just been laid off from Portland's Department of Health COVID-19 Investigation Team.

Marty did not know that back when Karen was practicing animal medicine, on the Northern wall of her office, there was a gigantic mural, you guessed it, a unicorn that Karen comedically named EAZY.

You literally can't make this stuff up. It is hard for me to say, as it will be hard for Marty to read when he finally gets the courage to buy this book, UNICORNS DO NOT EXIST ON THE EARTH ANY LONGER.

THEN THERE IS YOU

Before you close this book and donate it to Goodwill, let us look at something a little more exciting: you.

I bet you love the Bible, and you appreciate the Old Testament. You enjoy reading about the sacred sights. They remind you of the tour you took to Israel back in 2005. You love the idea of the earth's locations where humans experienced supernatural encounters with the living God. You devoured the stories about the miracles of Jesus, the exploits of the apostles, and the wonders of the early church fathers. You read about the church's history replete with manifestations of glory, and yet there is more. You are hungry and thirsty for encounters – yes! – but it's more than that. You don't want to be a Christian, in name only. You want to be a part of a world terraforming movement desiring to participate in the restoration of God's original plan until the planet resembles heaven.

Occasionally, in the twinkling of an eye, you see the twenty-first-century religious patterns abruptly interrupted by first-century power. Captured and enthralled by the moment, you watch the resurrection power of the Ancient of Days tearing the pages of the present, disrupting, shaking, and awakening everything!

However, during the seasons of outpouring, a subtle nagging voice whispers, "Don't get too excited." Amid the most incredible glory frenzies, we are taunted by the fear that history will inevitably repeat itself by something human interfering with this moment. What was once glorious is backtracking in time when humans engaged in lifeless, man-controlled worship and suffocating tradition.

The divine interpolations throughout church history are often referred to as revivals. Some of you may cringe when hearing that word because it reminds you of the past revival meetings that appeared contrived and powerless. For others, the word triggers an array of painful memories of expectations that eventually sputtered and died, making the heart sick.

Rumors have it that revivals don't exist. They are unicorns cooked up by the illusions of ministers drinking cherry slushies. I heard one minister say, "There is no such thing as revival." That secretly hurt my feelings because my church is called Seattle Revival Center. He was essentially saying that my church should change its name to Seattle Unicorn Center.

But I have a secret for you. Come closer and let me whisper in your ear. That minister is a fool. Revivals are not unicorns. They are portals, and *they exist*.

PORTAL TECH

Portals are gateways, doors that open and close. They are passageways offering immediate transportation from one realm to another. While on the island of Patmos, John saw a portal, an open door in heaven, and he was invited up to see the future. *After these things I looked, and behold, a door standing open in heaven, and the first voice which I had heard, like the sound of a trumpet speaking with me, said, "Come up here, and I will show you what must take place after these things* (Revelation 4:1, NASB).

The Greek word for door is *thyra,* meaning vestibule, folding door, entryway, passageway, and portal. There are times when a portal conducts you into a heavenly realm, and you see and hear amazing things. Other times, a portal is supernaturally opened in our realm, and we are flooded with unexpected opportunities and sometimes resistance. *For a wide door stands open before me which demands great efforts, and we have many opponents* (1 Corinthians 16:9, Weymouth New Testament).

Portals can immediately swallow you up in a lame meaningless life and then spit you out smack dab in the middle of an adventure carved out by a revelation of your new and true identity. When a portal opens, it makes a deafening screaming sound, "*Waaaaaaaa Waaaaaa!*" It is most frightening and yet ironically welcoming.

Portals are everywhere. If you don't believe me, ask your child. The older we get, the more our dreams of infinite possibilities can diverge into rationalist thinking that blinds us from the realities in the unseen world. Complacency and apathy can get the best of us, and tradition can become the end of us.

Just when you feel destined to live the rest of your life as a fisherman, then one day, a man named Jesus comes walking your way and invites you to attend his History Maker University. Jesus has a way of opening doors to the unforeseen coming attractions in your life. Jesus said, "I am the door," and he is the ultimate portal that offers a relationship instigating perpetual adventure, keeping you on the edge of your seat, never knowing what is next.

Excuse me, but I got ahead of myself. Follow me back to the beginning of all things in the book of Genesis. Since the fall of man, our sinister enemy has done his dastardly best to keep humanity from returning to the garden, where we enjoy the daily walks with God. As humanity wrestles with guilt and shame, they grapple with a paralyzing awareness of sin that prevents them from the life destined for them. Sin consciousness is like a cruel magician who tricks us into believing that our sin has zipped up the veil, like an old tent, closing the portal between us and God, therefore preventing our return to Eden.

What if there was an open portal like a magical wardrobe that leads us back to Narnia? What if it was possible to cross over into another world under God's government and a new heavenly atmosphere where you can breathe new life? And what if, like Dr. Ransom in C.S. Lewis' book, Perelandra, you could travel back in time to Eden's garden and kickstart the history of the world?

Every children's tale contains some sort of portal, another world where everything changes and is filled with adventure. As children, we are told that dreams do come true and that we are born with destiny in our blood, but then life happens, time flies by, and we end up spending forty hours in a cubicle world next to a gal named Sally who wrestles with a chronic runny nose.

What if your future didn't involve spending the rest of your life trying to gain the approval of a narcissistic manager that is hardly old enough to drive? What if a life of unending adventure, beauty, purity, and justice was not a myth? What if the Kingdom of God was more exciting than a Harry Potter novel? What if the church was more than just a boring weekly event hosted by an overly confident millennial with sinfully tight jeans? What if someone was knocking at your door, and when you opened the door, Jesus was staring you in the face, and then he said, "Come follow me."

LET ME INTRODUCE MYSELF

My name is Darren Jonathan Stott, and this is my story. I'm an overly confident millennial pastor who says "dude" way too often, and I am stinkin' passionate about portals. I am passionate about them because my grandpa got saved and called into ministry because of a revival portal. My dad was saved, called into ministry, and healed of stuttering, all because of a revival portal. Likewise, I was called into ministry because of, you guessed it, a revival portal. I am who I am because of portals. I have seen them open, and I have seen them close, and I've seen what happens to people who attempt to enter Narnia without the wardrobe. They die. Not literally. They die internally.

When you have seen the raw power of God and have felt the overwhelming and almost crippling weight of His glory, and you find yourself attempting to do ministry without it, like a police officer, with a gun but no bullets, it leaves you feeling dead inside.

EVERY PERSON NEEDS AN ENCOUNTER

Every person needs a Holy Spirit intrusion causing you to yearn to hear God's still small voice. Your soul secretly longs for defining moments so profound your identity is altered forever. Such memorable encounters of the supernatural illuminate the present and unwrap the future with meaning and motivation. These divine encounters provoke a spiritual deconstruction followed by a reconstruction under the soul-searching light of the Father's gaze. Living in the higher elevations, you gain a fresh perspective about life's purpose.

Your eternal purpose is interwoven into your DNA coded with exceptional skills and desires to realize a particular plan for your life. You are the living poetry of God. Designed by grace, you emerge into a person of mercy, stimulated to do justice while walking humbly before God.

If you haven't had your big bang moment, the awakening experience will amplify perception and sensitivity and intensify your awareness of your Christ-centered identity. If you long for these divine encounters, then this book was meant for you.

Every one of us needs a face-to-face encounter with the presence of God that frees us from a season of spiritual drought. How do you accumulate past revelations and experiences and convert them into a platform that launches you into the heavenly realm? Hunger and thirst are keys to destiny's door.

Hunger and thirst are natural human desires and are essential to your physical health. If you lose your appetite, it is an indication that something is wrong. It is the same spiritually. When there is no hunger for God's presence, it is indicative that something is wrong spiritually. In his book, *Deepening Your Conversation with God*, Ben Patterson draws a picture of how satisfaction diminishes your hunger for God. "We have become satisfied with a mere church, mere religious exertion, mere numbers and buildings—the things we can do. There is nothing wrong with these things, but they are no more than foam left by the surf on the ocean of God's glory and goodness."[1]

As the deer pants for the water brooks, so pants my soul for You, O God (Psalm 42:1). The eagerness and fervency of desire for God motivate you to arise and ascend into the high places where hunger and thirst are satisfied in the presence of God. The longing desire for God is at the very root of your spiritual well-being. There is no desire of the soul more intense than the heart has for God; there is no ache more deeply felt than what is experienced when one who loves God is cut off, creating spiritual isolation. Amid that dark night, can you hear the call to come to the water?

> *And Jesus said*
> *Come to the water*
> *Stand by My side*
> *I know you are thirsty*
> *You won't be denied*
> *I felt ev'ry tear drop*
> *When in darkness you cried*
> *And I strove to remind you*
> *That for those tears I died*[2]

An encounter with God is not supposed to be like milk, a limited quantity of a substance that will sour if not consumed by its expiration date. You never have to throw out a God encounter. In fact, every encounter is an everlasting portal, an entry point into the kingdom of heaven, leading to amazing adventures with the Father.

A POST-PORTAL ERA

In the Lion, Witch, and Wardrobe, there is a scene when Lucy realizes the portal did not open all the time because when she returned and tried to show the other children, they bumped against an ordinary wardrobe with a solid back. Sometimes, life feels like we live in a post-portal era as if the supernatural is no longer within humanities' reach. Two thousand years ago, the love of Christ carved out a realm by offering his life on a splintered cross. At the moment he surrendered his spirit, a cosmic tear occurred, ripping the veil in two, thus forever granting access to his sons and daughters.

And Jesus cried out again with a loud voice and yielded up his spirit. And behold, the curtain of the temple was torn in two, from top to bottom. And the earth shook, and the rocks were split (Matthew 27:50-51). The moment Jesus died, the veil was torn, and the wardrobe was opened forever to the heavenly realms!

WINE REPLACED WITH GRAPE DRINK

The problem is not that we live in a post-portal, post-revival, post-supernatural era. The new wine of the Spirit is freely available for you and me to receive and enjoy. We have replaced the new wine of the Spirit with mixture and compromise while substituting the wine of the Spirt with grape drink. It's not even grape juice; it's a disgusting grape drink composed of corn fructose, sugar, more sugar, grape-flavored syrup, and purple food dye. The disastrous substitute leaves a bitter taste in your mouth and drives people away from His presence.

There is no shortage of new wine!! Jesus is the new and living wine, and He has not withheld Himself from anyone. Jesus gave Himself entirely to his church and made his presence fully accessible through the Holy Spirit. The problem isn't with the quantity of wine but instead with the number of wineskins. Desperation surrounds us, and we need communities with the flexibility, ferocity, and theology to awaken people to their identity and destiny in Christ Jesus.

A NEW WINESKIN

Winemaking requires fermentation. I'm not a scientist or professional winemaker, so I will use laymen's terms to describe the process. Fermenting is when oxygen is allowed to mix with crushed fruit, water, and yeast. The yeast eats the sugars and converts them into alcohol. The fermenting process must be closely measured because once the fermenting is complete, it must be strained and then placed into a dark container and robbed of all oxygen. If the wine is not immediately transferred into an appropriate wineskin, the process goes in the wrong direction. Rather than turning water into wine, the wine turns into sour vinegar.

Winemaking requires an understanding of timing and processes and a diversity of vessels that serve various purposes. I'm not a cynical guy, but we must address the problems of stewarding opportunities afforded us at unexpected times. The crisis is not an absence of wine; it is the absence of thirst. If you are thirsty, it means you are not participating in the wine. Drinking the wine of the Spirit is a metaphor illustrating the importance of meditating on Christ, our eternal fountain of life. Drinking from the heavenly vats of God's Spirit satisfies the thirsty soul.

This book is written for those who have been crushed, transformed, purified, and shelved. The heavens and the earth have waited for your unveiling.

WHAT'S THE PLAN THEN?

You must understand how to carve out a realm where a move of God can be sustained in your home, your business, and your church. In this book, I will introduce the importance of carving out six principles that will help you protect the anointing on your life and the movement of the Spirit within this generation.

So, do you desire to be a catalyst for a vibrant presence-oriented community where the good news of the gospel is preached, producing Christlike righteousness, peace, and joy in the Holy Spirit? Great, but I know what you are wondering, "What's the plan?" The plan consists of carving out a revival culture with six disciplines. Though most millennials are allergic to the word, discipline is a potent truth. Discipline is the fierce commitment that involves consistent practice until a breakthrough occurs and a different realm of reality is carved out. These spiritual disciplines are customs of devotion practiced by God's people since the beginning of biblical times. Disciplines are not attitudes; they are practices like meditation, worship, reading, and writing.

The Apostle Paul disciplined himself to write. Under the heavy load of establishing the kingdom of God on earth, he still made time to write thirteen books for the churches he loved. I'm sorry to tell you this, but a scribe angel didn't write all those letters. He did it the tedious and old fashion with paper, quill, and ink. The human race survived because Noah had a solid work ethic and some discipline to finish the God-given project. Where we are today is founded on the discipline and passion of the preceding generations.

I'm a *finished-work-guy*, but I'm perhaps different from some of the other *finished-worked-guys*. My theology is this. In the garden, before the curse, God said, "Get to work." Then sin occurred, and everything got messed up. After Jesus died and was resurrected, he said, "It is finished. I've done my part. Now get back to work." John Wesley and many others believed as described in Edith Blumhofer's writings. "The state of entire sanctification allowed the believer to turn his or her attention outward toward the advancement of the gospel. In contrast, the state of partial sanctification was said to turn the believer's attention to the interior spiritual struggle for holiness which in turn limited his or her usefulness to the church and society."[3] *Such were some of you; but you were washed, but you were sanctified, but you were justified in the name of the Lord Jesus Christ and in the Spirit of our God* (1 Corinthians 6:11, NASB).

It's time for us to work, not for salvation and sanctification, or to get closer to Jesus, and not in fear of rejection from people. It's time for us to get to work because we know we are saved, we know we are in union with Jesus, and we know that rejection cannot define us. We are loved so we should live like we are accepted, loved, and well-raised children of God. We were created in the image and likeness of a hard-working God, a committed Trinity that is fully invested in the restoration of all things.

Conversely, living dependent on the Father in everything, he worked for God. He did whatever he saw the Father doing (John 5:19). They worked in harmony with each other, and so should we.

This book is an explanation and an invitation to join me in following the six disciplines. None of these practices are gifts, and none are accomplished by the finished work of the cross; it's done by you working while empowered by the Spirit.

Jesus accomplished the mission predetermined by the Father, and now the world deserves that we build a platform of moral consistency and excellence that manifests Christ to the world. In the past, some moves of God were thwarted by those who did not foresee or could marry grace with discipline. The two are not foes; they are joined at the hip.

THE SIX DISCIPLINES

1. Expectation
2. Preparation
3. Communication
4. Collaboration
5. Celebration
6. Evaluation

CARVING OUT A REALM

Revival doesn't just happen. It takes discipline, hard work, and heaps of grace. Applying these values will not help if you are just looking for some hacks to pop off a good glory meeting. This book is for those who are seriously vested and rooted in a community that values the moving of the Spirit.

If you are not in such a community, but you desire to be, then we can labor together to create, sustain, and protect the momentum manifested through our partnership with the Father. The word Patricia King chose for this process is called "carving out."

I once had a dream where it felt like we had arrived as a church. It was like, "Wow, I am the pastor of The Seattle Revival Center. Awesome!" In the dream, a man criticizes and accuses me of not doing anything to create and sustain the momentum, and he assumed I was some sort of spoiled trust-fund baby. I was so mad, I put my index finger into his chest, and I said, "You have NO idea what you are saying. We have worked, labored, invested, prayed, and stewarded what the Lord has given us to be where we are." I woke up shaking.

I know the price I paid, and the meticulous, painstaking work needed to create Kingdom communities that bring heaven to earth and the culture's vitalization. I refuse to partner with adrenaline-addicted experience seekers who track glory clouds like the cable-TV ghost hunters.

I don't want to hear things from ministers saying, "Let's blow it up," unless they refer to target practice with Tannerite. Do you want MORE of God? Do you know why or what is at stake, and what is it worth to you? Do you understand what it might cost your families, churches, and regions if you choose counterfeits instead of the real deal? Our generation has an opportunity to carve out a revival realm in the world cultures, locations where heaven invades and abides on earth. The question isn't if God is willing? The question is. Are you ready? Will you accept Father's invitation to step into the wardrobe and enter the possibilities associated with Father's world?

It's time to carve.

CHAPTER TWO

CARVING OUT A CULTURE OF EXPECTATION

"As it is my eager expectation and hope that I will not be at all ashamed, but that with full courage now as always Christ will be honored in my body, whether by life or by death."
—Philippians 1:20, ESV

WE WERE STANDING in line again, but this time it wasn't for the *Honey I Shrunk the Kids* 4D experience at EPCOT. That was yesterday. Today was a new day, and we were in line to go to a revival meeting. The people at the front of the line had arrived when the sun was still rising, and yet, every forty-five minutes, in the scorching sun, they still possessed the energy to spontaneously break out singing the chorus of Look What the Lord Has Done, while hopping around like bunny rabbits.

I waited alongside my mom and dad, not knowing what all the buzz what about, but there was buzz; everybody was buzzing with expectation. Waiting in long lines to go to church wasn't a foreign thing to do during this time; this was the tail end of a four-year period where revivals were breaking out everywhere. We had stood in all kinds of lines, from waiting outside the Langley Vineyard for the Randy Clark meetings to standing in line to get into Rodney Howard Browne camp meetings. Luckily in Toronto, John and Carol Arnott would sneak us in the side door. Finally, the crowd began to cheer and move; the doors had been opened. In front of me, a skinny man began to hoe-down with expectancy as his mullet caught wind of the spirit and began to pull him and his denim shorts towards the entrance. He was our beardless Moses.

In fifty-eight seconds, twenty-five hundred people flooded the sanctuary. The atmosphere felt radioactive, like 5G-radioactive, yet that wouldn't be rolled out for another twenty-five years. The atmosphere was alive, and during this time, the pre-meeting atmosphere was almost a litmus test to determine whether or not a move of God was legit or not. It didn't matter what revival stream you belonged to; you always knew it was going to pop when you would get a whiff of that pre-meeting expectancy.

I wondered what sort of meeting this was going to be. We had experienced all of the revival cultures up to this point. Toronto Airport Vineyard was my favorite. It was like a 1960's Californian beach revival, except in Canada. No matter what was happening on the stage, most of the people either danced around the room or laid on the ground son gazing. Rodney Howard Brown meetings were like a Men's Warehouse corporate Christmas party. Grown men would stagger, sing while staggering, and sometimes rip off their ties and shoes and run around the room, only to slow down, stagger, and fall to the ground, all while wearing black suits. Vineyard conferences were like meditation retreats where the Holy Ghost would frequently pull out a hand grenade and blow up half the room. It didn't usually detract from the message. If you didn't get blown up, you would take notes and patiently wait your turn. You would inevitably get obliterated before the night was done.

It was 7:00 PM, and our meeting was beginning. I was expecting the worship to sound like the church's red carpet and pews, but it hit hard and loud. "Look what the Lord has done," exploded in the room. The people from outside must have been prophetic. We were off like Nascar, and I was digging it.

I repented to the Lord for stereotyping AG worship; this wasn't a Gaither gathering. It felt more like a James Brown concert (except with mostly white people). The funky bass player slapped his strings, the eighteen to twentysomethings swayed in the choir, and five female vocalists worshiped the Lord with their hands and hair, reaching high up into the third Heaven where Jesus sits.

Finally, the pastor got up to preach. Well, I thought he was the pastor. The real pastor invited this guy to preach on Father's Day, June 18th, 1995, and it was so good that he never left. This guy could preach. He preached, he preached, and he preached until the atmosphere could no longer handle it. The room felt like John Jacob's water bottle one second away from exploding. This little girl ran out on the stage and started belting out a song about mercy. The preacher was like, "You better get up! You better get saved right now! Get out of the balcony," he must have known we were up there; we had been found out, " Repent of your sins and receive forgiveness. Come and kneel at these altars be washed clean."

Hundreds of people began running to the altars, including my dad. I was confused, my dad was a second-generation pastor who signed a denominational covenant to abstain from all appearances of sin, including but not limited to frequenting movie theatres, listening to secular music, and anything to do with cocaine. Right before my very eyes my sinless dad was running to the altar to get saved. I remember thinking, "Gosh, if there's sin in his life, I'm screwed." I ran behind him to the front of the church. On our knees we wept, father and son, at the altars of the Brownsville Revival, and I am proud to say that on that very night, I received Jesus as my personal Lord and savior, for the three hundredth time.

When I think back on the on buttery atmospheres of revival in the '90s, I always remember palatable corporate expectancy; an expectancy that fills like a buzz, like electricity, like gas invisibly collecting in the air just waiting for a spark. When people begin to gather to be in the presence of God when there is a conviction that when we gather something Heavenly is going to occur, this corporate expectation creates a magnet for Heaven, where the manifest fire of God consumes the holy desire of His people. We say come; Lord Jesus come!

In the psychology of expectation, merely expecting something to happen does not make it happen necessarily. Cultural hype can conjure up fleeting hope, but according to my detailed analysis, manipulated expectation leads to disappointment about eighty-nine-point seven percent of the time. When God is moving in power, an atmosphere of faith is established; a corporate knowing that God is present, and that big things are not only possible but probable.

I have walked into meetings at Seattle Revival Center, and before a prayer could be prayed or a guitar strummed, there was an undeniable energy in the room. The atmosphere generates expectation, creates unity, and leads to an explosion of praise and worship. Sometimes, I have experienced kinetic energy in places where revival was not necessarily their core value. You do not have to be a revival center to encounter a revival atmosphere. Whenever God shows up, things change, no matter the place or circumstances. The factor that determines consistent expectancy is the word "culture." Culture is the wineskin by which experiences, beliefs, and behavior are framed. Every community has its unique culture.

For example, consider the culture of a family. When I enter someone's home, I can discern the family culture, not judge them, and honor and serve their cultural expectations. A family's culture may have boundaries I should respect. For instance, when you arrive at someone's house, you may see mountains of shoes at the front door. It is indicative of a cultural expectation and boundary; the shoes are communicating the expectation of the culture. Even if I am told I can wear my shoes, I will honor the culture and contribute my Air Jordan's to the family's Mt. Everest that blocks passage to their home.

Our cultures reveal our positive and negative expectations. Many families have a morning culture or an evening one. There could be a Sunday morning culture, a Monday night culture, or a Friday night culture. Sometimes, these cultures can excuse negative behaviors; for example, if I ignore my family every Monday morning, this act of selfishness will eventually create an unspoken dysfunctional culture to which my family will eventually submit. The kids might even say, "Don't talk to dad because it's MONDAY morning." Over time, negative behaviors can create deeply ingrained dysfunctional patterns; patterns that over time stretch out the fibers of our relationship and intimacy.

We can get away with stuff at home that anywhere else would be unacceptable, but because the behavior is private, it becomes acceptable, but only on Monday mornings because that is the culture that was created.

Experiences can alter expectations. Our cultures create subconscious expectations. For example, many families have a holiday expectation, and with that culture, a series of negative expectations can precede the holidays. Subconscious negative expectations framed by consistent negative experiences become principalities of thought that begin to rule over the holidays.

FAITH AND EXPECTATIONS

Before we take a plunge into this topic, it is essential to understand the biblical meaning and perspective concerning expectation. The International Standard Bible Encyclopedia covers the New Testament, and Strong's Hebrew covers the Hebrew words for expectation. First, a quote from the Greek.

"Of the three Greek words, translated in the New Testament "expect," *prosdokao* means to look forward toward what will probably occur, whether in hope or dread (see Acts 3:5 Luke 3:15); it is not as intense as the second Greek word *ekdechomai* (Hebrews 10:13) that means to wait for that of the realization of which one is assured; it is not as vivid as the noun *apokaradokia* (Romans 8:19 Philippians 1:20) meaning "earnest expectation," which describes the stretching forth of the head toward an object that is anticipated."[4]

Of the various Hebrew words, one of the prominent ones that relate to this chapter are three Hebrew words, *tochleth*, *seber*, and *tiqvah* which all are translated with the word hope.

Jentezen Franklin sheds light on the two, dynamic faith and the power of expectation, and God is the source and stimulator. "Our God is all-powerful, yet we limit His work in our lives when we refuse to believe in His ability and His victory. We need to activate our faith and stand in tiptoe expectation, knowing He can do the impossible!"[5]

I gave you only negative examples of the influence of dysfunctional cultures and subconscious expectations to illustrate how powerful and dangerous expectation can be, and yes, expectation is dangerous because it's not just a natural thought process. Expectation can empower belief, and belief is what locks and unlocks the supernatural.

In John 3:16, Jesus said, "...*whosoever believes in me will not perish.*" Jesus is saying that if we reframe our expectations by refocusing through the filter of Christ's lordship, the natural consequences of decay-based expectations will be supernaturally replaced with eternal expectations resulting in abundant life and immortality. At this point, the combination of expectations generated by faith morphs from the natural to the supernatural, from a mere desire to dangerous faith. Genuine Christianity gets activated by the culture of heaven when a strong inherent belief becomes our default thought, the belief that it is the will of God to manifest Himself through His Church here and now. Therefore, inevitably, something will happen because **we are here**, engaging and partnering with God's will, and ready to be escorted to abundant life and bringing shalom to all the Earth.

I've heard some Christians say they don't have a lot of faith. I always challenge people on that statement. I tell them that they have lots of faith; it's just negative faith. Let's get back to the Monday example. If we attach a negative expectancy to Monday, then we will get what we expect. That tired, lethargic, unmotivated feeling will always show up on Mondays because we have a strong negative belief attached to that day.

NO EXPECTATIONS, NO DISAPPOINTMENT

Alexander Pope is well known for saying, "Blessed is he who expects nothing, for he shall never be disappointed." Perhaps you would say, "Darren, I don't have positive expectations or negative expectations. I do not want to be disappointed, and so I do not expect anything. That way, I will be pleasantly delighted if something good happens." Honestly, I've heard so many Christians say this, and my response is simple, Hebrews 11:6, *"Without faith, it's impossible to please God."*

No expectation is a negative expectation. When we make a choice "not to believe," it is often because we are anchored to a past moment where a positive expectation led to a major disappointment. After being let down, perhaps you thought, "I will never allow myself to be let down like that, ever again." When we lose our sense of expectation, with it, we lose our sense of excitement and adventure. When there is no expectation, it is an indicator that our intimacy is threatened by a hopeless and joyless tradition. Listen, I'm not anti-tradition, but I am anti joyless tradition. If there's no joy in it, then maybe, what was once hot has become lukewarm.

If there's no expectancy in your weekly date night, then there's no creativity that night. Sometimes tradition, while holding us accountable, costs us our passionate, creative investment.

Why do you do what you do? Do you do it only because it's on your calendar? Maybe it's time to re-evaluate your commitments; check the thermometer, and see if you are hot, cold, or lukewarm?

. . .

EVERY TIME WE MEET

When we carve out a realm of revival, we must use the culture of expectation to interlace with the fabric of our influence. **Every time we gather, there is an opportunity for God to show up and show off.**

In Matthew 18:20, Jesus basically says, "Every time you gather, gather with expectancy, because every time you meet, my manifest presence will meet with you." What if, at every time we gathered as a family, a church, a home group, or a Bible Study, we expected to encounter Jesus? What if, at every gathering, there was a manifestation of Jesus? We would have to start selling tickets.

EXPECTATION, THE MOTHER OF MANIFESTATION

My good friend, Pastor Greg Daley, once said, "Expectation is the mother of manifestation." Expectation doesn't just happen. The big, bold, bodacious expectation is a fruit of good theology. When we don't expect much from God, usually it is because subconsciously we have believed a sequence of lies, lies such as, "We aren't in a season of revival," or "Making God show up is too much work, so we'll just resort to the easy route and teach and equip people."

If we do not see manifestations of the presence of Jesus, I can assure you it is not because He is not present. His promise to never leave us nor forsake us is a theological slap on the bum of those who do not expect Jesus to appear. What Jesus is saying is, "I am with you now and forever. Live your lives as though you believe I am with you and for you."

When we don't have expectation, we develop systems that don't require God's presence for their success. Any system that exists to reveal Jesus, and yet does not require the Holy Spirit is worth disassembling.

At Seattle Revival Center, we developed a preaching series called, "God is here!" The purpose of the series was to develop a theology and a culture of expectation, a dependency on the always present presence of Holy Spirit. We created a promotional video with three scenes, where a man was sitting in traffic, and a mom was pushing a grocery cart through the grocery store with three screaming babies, and a couple was arguing in their bedroom. With each scene, we declared, "God is here!"

For too long we have allowed our feelings to be our Holy Spirit detector, but our soul makes a lousy barometer to gauge God's presence in the room. God's unchanging word is the document revealing the reality and availability of the Holy Spirit at any given moment. 1 Corinthians 6:19 says, "'*Or do you not know that your body is a temple of the Holy Spirit within you, whom you have from God?*"

It's funny, I used to be a worship leader, and there was another leader in our church who tried to teach me the songs Holy Spirit really liked. He informed me that specific songs attract Holy Spirit. That wasn't weird to hear. It was sort of like unspoken Pneumatology (the study of the Holy Spirit). It appears that Holy Spirit is like Casper the Ghost except he has no eyes or mouth, just two colossal elephant ears, and He's like the biggest music snob in the world, and so you better play His favorite songs, or He'll abandon the Earth forever.

Listen, if you are in Christ, Holy Spirit is in you. You do not need to sing, scream, beg, and dance to get Him to come. That's what the false prophets of Baal did to get their false God to ignite the altar. Expectation is the key. We believe in the faithfulness of His word; therefore, He manifests Himself through the confidence of His children.

I believe it is time for us to confront the pieces of our cultures that enable cold, systematic behaviors void of intimacy, fire, and partnership with the Trinity.

CARVING OUT YOUR CULTURE OF EXPECTANCY

What is the level of expectancy in the atmosphere of which you are a part? One way you can begin to carve out a culture of expectation is to create an expectancy chart in your journal. Craft your title, and then underneath, design a scoring system, 1 – 10. One means no expectancy, and ten means highly expectant. For example:

YOUR MARRIAGE:

1 2 3 4 5 6 7 8 9 10

COLD   HOT

WHY:

_____

_____

_____

WHAT CAN CHANGE?

1. _____

2. _____

3. _____

Assessing the expectancy of the culture and environment we are leading is an opportunity to collect valuable data and communicate our vision and future desire to cultivate an atmosphere shifting expectations to the present moment. Dreaming is contagious. As we begin to involve people in the process of confronting the mundane, the expectation will breakthrough into other people's hearts.

If you are hosting a homegroup, you could ask the attendants a question like, "When you come here on Wednesday nights, assess what level of expectation you have, and how could we increase our corporate expectation, so we see greater measures of a breakthrough when we gather?"

Write down the feedback, repeat the feedback, and praise those who dared to speak. Try not to interrupt people while going through the process, and whatever you do, refuse to be offended by the feedback. Reject the temptation to offer excuses because things are the way they are.

Many leaders refuse to ask for feedback because they fear the data could be incriminating. If it stings, you know it is working. If it is not fair or a morale booster, try to find a way to take responsibility for your insight, and promise to seek counsel from both the Lord and others as you process what's been shared.

Data is so overwhelming for me. At Seattle Revival Center, it's almost impossible for me to find strategic solutions based on data alone without processing through it with a few trusted peers. Over coffee, we can assess the priority of the problems we discovered and attempt to extract the Holy Ghost opportunities. Not to be redundant, but problems are opportunities for growth, and they are not judging the leadership. Rejoice when you discover an unseen problem because you found a hidden key.

WE ARE EXPECTING

When Andrea and I learned we were expecting our first child, and we chose not to share it with anybody for the first three months. Even though we didn't say anything, the people close to us and familiar with our atmosphere knew we were expecting. Our positive expectation carved out a discernable and contrasting atmosphere. People knew our secret because our expectations spoke louder than words.

The secret expectation between Andrea and I also carved out a new level of intimacy. We knew that our lives were about to change forever, and the expected change brought us together as we began communicating and, you guessed it, preparing!

CHAPTER THREE

PREPARATION

"By failing to prepare, you are preparing to fail."
—Benjamin Franklin

GET READY! CHANGE IS IN THE AIR

THE BIRTH OF our first child was exciting, but it involved immediate attention to unforeseen logistics. Of course, there were the obvious things to prepare for; however, there are always surprises that required a response. Decision-making was a little more complicated. It was no longer how our decisions impacted two people; now, it affected three, from small things like Andrea's reducing caffeine intake to getting serious and finding our first home. We had no choice. To stay ahead of the curve, we resolved to be militant in our preparation because we were expecting a child.

In 2018 and 2019, we heard the Lord tell the Seattle Revival Center, "Get ready, you are expecting." As a church community, before you realized it, we experienced a literal baby boom. All sorts of couples in the church, including Anthony and Rebekah (our Associate Pastors), and Andrea and I learned that we were expecting our fourth child. Not only that, but the church was growing, and our children's ministries had escalated.

There's an intriguing maxim that continues to shock me to this day. It is found in 1 Corinthians 15:46. *However, the spiritual is not first, but the natural, and afterward the spiritual.* Archibald Robertson called it the law of progress and development. But there is more to the ancient adage. We can quickly shift from maxims to signs. So, the baby boom was a sign of the future church growth. Even as our family prepared for our fourth child, our church prepared for the spiritual children coming. If you are wise, you understand that expectation is quickly joined to preparation. The spiritual equation is obvious; expectation plus preparation leads to spiritual success.

GODS SECRET PLANS REVEALED

Andrea discovered she was pregnant when the plus sign appeared on a pregnancy test. An external indicator of an internal shift was our alarm bell for the imminent transition.

Prophesy reveals the secrets of the Father's workshop. Even now, Jesus is intimately interweaving the secret parts for an increase in God's Kingdom, and it was never His intention to withhold the secrets. Amos 3:7 says, "*Surely the Lord GOD does nothing, Unless He reveals His secret to His servants the prophets.*" This means God does nothing without first a declaration or prophetic revealing. God spoke, and heaven kissed the earth, light dissipated the darkness, and His secrets were revealed to His friends, the prophets.

This truth is modeled in Genesis 1. In the beginning, God said, "Let there be light." The word God spoke precipitated the creative work. First, the word and then the act. In Psalms 107:20, David alluded to this principle when he says, *He sent His word and healed them.*

Likewise, throughout His ministry, Jesus adhered to this precedent. He made a declaration before carrying out the supernatural manifestation. Matthew 8:16 illustrates this spiritual reality. *And He cast out the spirits with a word and healed all who were sick.*

Hearing heaven first and then responding by action is key to human activity. Hearing the divine word is the pathway to creative effort. So, the required faith and blueprint to effectively prepare the way is accessible through first hearing God. Like the wind, good ideas come and go, but completing God's ideas requires conviction, commitment, and administration.

I am continually honored and humbled when the Lord shares with me the words He is scribing in the heavenly realm for manifestation and transformation in the earthly realm. 1 Corinthians 2:9-10 says, *"But, as it is written, "What no eye has seen, nor ear heard, nor the heart of man imagined, what God has prepared for those who love him"*— these things God are revealed to us through the Spirit. In 1 Corinthians 2:10, Paul writes that the Spirit searches everything, even the depths of God. It pleases the Lord to reveal His secret plans to his friends. I love how Jesus puts it in John 15:15, *"No longer do I call you servants, for the servant does not know what his master is doing; but I have called you friends, for all that I have heard from my Father I have made known to you."*

The kind of prophetic revelation needed to carve out a revival realm in your region or sphere will require this kind of friendship. Many people scurry around like confused mice, traveling from conference to conference, looking for a prophetic word, but the word you need to hear comes through friendship with the Creator.

Psalms 25:14 puts it like this, *"The friendship of the LORD is for those who fear him, and he makes known to them his covenant."* Interlaced in this verse is a beautiful double bind, a wild predicament, baffling the mind and stimulating the spirit: without intimacy with God, it is impossible to partner with Him, and yet devoid of partnering with Him, it is impossible to enjoy intimacy with God. Remember, God's desired outcome is not the ultimate intention. Partnering together and preparing with the Father for intimacy with God is ultimately the divine purpose. I refuse to do anything for God that involves doing something without Him.

PREPARATION REQUIRES ADMINISTRATION

At the end of 2015, the Lord spoke to me and said, "Darren, you are doing local church well, but I've called you to be a revival center." Upon hearing that word, I immediately called all our elders and planned for an elders' retreat at the beginning of 2016. As a result of the retreat, we experienced a unified commitment to partner together and administrated what the Father wanted to accomplish on the earth.

It empowered us with the grace to plan and implement extended revival meetings during February of 2016. We advertised three meetings a day that extended five weeks before setting a new pace that involved weekend meetings instead of daily sessions. I don't care if you are running daily meetings or weekend meetings because anything beyond weekly meetings requires excellent administration.

As an elder board, we agreed we were not willing for the local church to suffer at the expense of hosting a revival. We believed that with excellent administration, the local church would prosper by hosting the presence of the Lord. The intensity and unpredictability of revival shook us deeply. We saw our desires and the Father's desires being satisfied, and yet, we had no idea what we were doing or where we were going. This season was radically successful for us as a church, and not because we were radically strategic. We had a record number of newcomers connecting to the local church, our discipleship schools were packed out, and our connect groups had a record number of signups. All because our leadership team took administrative ownership of the process, meaning that we all worked together to host what God was doing.

. . .

THE VIOLENT ROCK-CUTTING RIVER OF GOD

The Columbia River Gorge is a canyon of the Columbia River in the Pacific Northwest of the United States. The canyon stretches up to four thousand feet deep for over eighty miles as the river winds westward through the Cascade Range. You should hear the geological theories on how it violently carved out this massive canyon.

What happened in 1994 and 2016 at Seattle Revival Center was not a result of us carving out a revival realm. These moves of God were sovereign rock-cutting torrents that carved out a cannon whereby a new river of life could flow. Revival isn't clean and neat; it's messy, chaotic, and certainly not orderly. There is no controlling the earth-modifying river of God's glory. When referencing administration, we are not talking about controlling a move of God; we are intentionally protecting the values of our communities, the pillars that God constructed, so we don't compromise the cellular structure of our divine DNA during the rollercoaster of emotions, and the changing tides that accompany trying to keep up with a moving God.

HOLD THE TENSION

I love the term "carving out a realm" because it communicates the process and maybe even the pain required to create a revival culture intentionally. Preparation for and the administration of revival dynamics is an invitation into a new and radical tension. A leader's role within these environments is not to eliminate tension but to recognize, discern, and then choose whether to defuse or embrace the tension.

Discerning the trajectory of tension involves determining whether or not the tension leads to a positive or negative end. One example of negative pressure is relational discord between two leaders. The division or misunderstanding could be an opportunity for the enemy to derail and maybe even deceive others.

Because the Kingdom of God consists of relationships and collaboration, the unwillingness to reconcile is a red flag, an indicator of pride. This negative tension must be addressed to protect the unity and testimony of Jesus Christ.

However, other types of tension do not need to be solved; they need to be held. For example, relational tension can exist between the pastor and the evangelist generated by the uniqueness of their calling and passion. During times of revival, the pastor may want to slow things and maybe even do fewer meetings because he feels the discipleship systems are not sufficient. People are not connecting, and perhaps, they are not going deeper in their relationship with the Lord. However, the evangelist may be deeply disturbed because each night, over a hundred people made commitments to Christ, and for the evangelist, the idea of "slowing down" seems insanely foolish.

This tension is terrific!! It should not be eliminated but both parties must learn how to allow the tension to be an opportunity to understand each other's perspective. The worse thing that can happen is that the pastor caves and say that his desire for depth is pointless, and in his insecurity, he abdicates his leadership because of the evangelist's charisma. Likewise, the evangelist should not shut down the revival and move on to the next church. These tensions engender occasions to be more intentional, efficient, and even more biblical.

Disagreement is only a problem when it leads to disunity. Part of expectancy and preparation for revival involves creating diverse environments where five-fold leadership can collaborate and carve the realm out together. Alone, one person is incapable of carving out a sustainable realm. Sustainability requires unity in vision and methodology, which means that we need synergistic leadership at the vision's point of origin.

. . .

PREPARE TO BE INCONVENIENCED

At the time of this writing, we were about three weeks away from having our fourth child, and during the night, Andrea was up several times. She could not sleep the night before, as well. I had just returned from Africa with my oldest daughter, Abigail, and I thought we would be the ones wrestling with jetlag, and instead, it seemed as though Andrea was the one with jetlag. Andrea would wake up every night, and because she was wide awake, she started doing household chores, like folding laundry, doing dishes, or even vacuuming, IN THE MIDDLE OF THE NIGHT!

I knew she was uncomfortable, but I couldn't figure out what was happening with her sleep habits, and it bothered me because when she wakes up, I wake up, and I don't like to wake up. Then I had an epiphany. Her body is preparing her for the future inconveniences of being a mommy. It's not just preparing her; it's preparing both of us.

For some reason, even though I know we were expecting, it did not occur that our whole lives were about to change *again*. This was a change so significant that the Lord placed preparation triggers within a mother's biology to prepare the parents for less sleep, to be alert and available to care for a new child.

There is no nice way to say this. Revival is the biggest inconvenience we will ever face. Revival forces us to re-evaluate all our priorities. Revival demands difficult conversations. Revival tests our gifts and callings because if we are not in the right place on the bus (as Jim Collins would say), then the intensity of revival could lead to burning out.

For some people, the intensity and inconvenience are reason enough not to go after the things of the Spirt. Some might say, "It is just too much work," or "It is way too messy." Does this sound familiar? In today's culture, many couples say the same thing regarding their choice not to have kids. David would caution us with these words, "If it cost us nothing, then it's not worth offering to the Lord" (see 1 Chronicles 21:24). Things worth doing well always require sacrifice, care, and investment. If you choose to birth God's dreams in your generation, I promise you will never regret the inconvenience.

PREPARATION SURVEY

Don't just read through these questions. Take the time to write out the answers in your journal or on a piece of notebook paper. Finishing this book isn't the win. Finding opportunities for heart-change along the way is where the value is revealed. Slow down and ask Holy Spirit to help you as we answer these questions:

1. What part of your heart is the Lord attempting to put His finger on?
2. Where are you apprehensive when you think about hosting His presence?
3. In what areas are you unwilling to pay the price to run with God's dreams in your life?
4. Why does the cost seem so significant?
5. What are the lies you believed regarding the adverse outcomes that accompany obeying God?
6. What negative tension do you need to resolve in this current season?
7. What positive tension do you need to hold?
8. What are the opportunities for collaboration and the available input within the positive tension?

CHAPTER FOUR

COMMUNICATION

*"The single biggest problem in communication
is the illusion that it has taken place."*
—*George Bernard Shaw*

CARVING OUT A DISCIPLINE OF COMMUNICATION

IF YOU ENDEAVOR together to create, steward, and sustain revival portals on earth, then you must carve out a discipline for communication. If your heart issues are the reason, you disappear or attack when feeling hurt or threatened, you weaken the foundation needed to not only survive within the church but thrive. The issues must be examined and healed before you can lead within the Body of Christ. The church has not scored well in the communication department, and now with the train-wreck known as social media, we can attack whoever without accountability or consequences.

Remember, revival is not the destination; it is the portal back to Eden realities of heaven on earth. It means that boisterous nightly events are not the win, but rather a vibrant, mystical union with God and man that terraforms the earth.

NO MORE LANGUAGE BARRIERS

As I sat next to my new friend on his leather couch, a smile spread across his face as he explained how he could speak sixteen different languages. The only language he studied was Hebrew because all the other languages were supernaturally downloaded in him by the Holy Spirit. My friend Shawn commented, "I need you to pray for me." He laughed a big, hearty contagious laugh and explained, "You just need the gift of understanding."

My new friend, Pastor Surprise Sithole, is from Nelspruit, South Africa, and yes, his name is Pastor Surprise. His name was supposed to be *Try* because his parents were "trying" to have a child for quite some time, but instead, his parents gave him the name Surprise after they were "surprised" to discover a grey patch of hair on his head when he was born.

A few days later, we met with Pastor Surprise, and this time for a podcast interview. I wanted to dive deeper into his revelation of language. During our conversation, Pastor Surprise explained to me that up until Genesis eleven all of humanity had the gift of understanding because they could communicate with each other. However, in Genesis 11:7, God said, "*Let us go down and confuse their language so they cannot communicate with each other.*" At this point, a data packet of misunderstanding was downloaded into the human genome (my paraphrase); however, in Acts 2, the Lord reversed the Genesis curse.

In Acts 2:11, the foreigners were perplexed by the recent Spirit-infused believers saying, "*...we hear them declaring the wonders of God in our own tongues!*" The gift of understanding filled the believers with the Holy Spirit, and they were able to share the gospel without any language barriers. Pastor Surprise speaks incredible English, and yes, he was "awakened" to the entire English language, as well!!

. . .

I THOUGHT YOU WERE A UNICORN,
AND YOU TURNED OUT TO BE A DONKEY

You are where you are because of the conversations you chose to have, or perhaps the conversations you were not willing to have. Perhaps you met the perfect woman, or the perfect man (a unicorn), and you found the perfect job, and finally, found the perfect church. Then over time, life happened, and you realized that the whole thing was a façade. Maybe you said something to yourself like, "The system is rigged. All _____ (fill in the blank) are stupid, and I'll never give my heart to _____ again."

The problem wasn't with women, men, the marketplace, or churches; the problem was diversity. Humans are an assortment of dissimilar personalities. For example, Andrea and I are radically different.

The human differences include our edges, passions, and experiences, which shape us in a specific way that sometimes causes difficulties in connecting, partnering, and communicating. For this reason, we must never assume that honest communication is easy or comes naturally. The more meaningful the relationship, the more challenging and vulnerable, and the rawer communication becomes.

Communication is easier when we have nothing to lose. Incredible opportunities for intimacy are thwarted when scared away by honesty and vulnerability in conversations. If it is hard, stressful, and scary, then most likely, it is worth it.

Without consistent and effective communication, your perspective of the other person will subtly shift in a downward spiral. For example, if a woman craftily manipulates the situation, the man might feel like he is being taken advantage of and then resists or retreats, but that is not the answer. Open and honest communication is the answer to such an uncomfortable situation. So, if the man opens his heart and shares his feelings of uneasiness or frustration with the circumstances, and then communicates why their relationship is important to him, this opens the door for her response. Now, she has the opportunity to explain herself and that she never intended to manipulate the situation; she was simply trying to resolve it. By taking this approach, he protected his honor and her identity.

It's easier to make a judgment against someone and cut them off rather than fight for the Father's perspective of who they are. Usually, the best way to deal with an incorrect judgment is to bring it into the light and appropriately process the issue with the person you are wrestling with. This is when the "Matthew 18 Principle" is appropriate. "When a brother or sister sins against you…" (Matthew 15:18, the Darren Stott translation).

When not *if*. It is not about *if* someone is going to sin against you, but rather, what are you going to do *when* they sin? Jesus would say, "Go directly to them, and attempt to work it out in private." Of course, if slime hits the fan and is not resolved, then go to step number two. Guess what, this is not easy, but it matters because we are talking about preserving and protecting a person's Christ identity within our heart's. How we see each other matters. We might say, "Nobody's perfect," but if we "know each other" according to the Spirit rather than the flesh, we should be able to see each other according to their identity in Christ rather than their shortcomings? You might think, "No way, that raises the bar too high!"

Exactly. What do we do if people are incapable of measuring up to the unrealistic standards? We remember grace. I didn't say tolerance. I said empowerment.

By demonstrating grace, we partner with one another to assist in their empowerment, and help them overcome the weakness while not dishing out fresh judgment against them. I am thankful when I fail because my heavenly Father does not see me as a failure. He comes near to me, loves me, gives me insight and revelation, and then authorizes me to try again. I want to be more like my Father, which means I must learn to keep my heart open, even when I feel betrayed. I don't know about you, but when I feel like trust has been violated, the line of communication is the first thing I shut down.

Let us imagine you found the wonderful woman, the ideal man (and he is shirtless, riding a unicorn, and has a Starbucks coffee for you), the perfect job, or the perfect church, and then something happens, and your perspective is challenged. What do you do? Again, I would encourage you to fight for the perspective of honor and ask yourself the question, "What will it take to preserve it?" Most likely, you will find God's grace is sufficient, and that honor really can be restored through honest, heartfelt, and nonreligious communication.

Restoration occurs when people are bold enough to be real, truthful, humble, and connect from the heart.

REVIVALS END WHEN PEOPLE STOP COMMUNICATING

When you study the historical record of revivals worldwide, we can find a pattern, a sequence of events that subverts the moves of God and closes the portal. When a revival ceases to exist, it is not because God has checked out and floated back up to heaven. Revival tarries when government crumbles. When I refer to government, I imply a wineskin of wisdom and godly rule, where spiritual authority brings peace and order within its jurisdiction. Everything has the possibility of being correctly governed, because we have been given authority and dominion by Christ to rule and bring shalom. *Then God said, "Let Us make man in Our image, according to Our likeness; and let them rule over the fish of the sea and over the birds of the sky and over the cattle and over all the earth, and over every creeping thing that creeps on the earth"* (Genesis 1:26).

And Jesus came and said to them, all authority in heaven and on earth has been given to me. Go therefore and make disciples of all nations, baptizing them in the name of the Father and of the Son and of the Holy Spirit" (Matthew 28:18-19).

In his book, *The Normal Christian Church Life*, Watchman Nee said that it is death to have a wineskin without wine, but it is a loss to have wine without a wineskin. We must have the wineskin after we have the wine.[6] In the parable of the wine and the wineskins, Jesus said, *"Nor do they put new wine into old wineskins, or else the wineskins break, the wine is spilled, and the wineskins are ruined. But they put new wine into new wineskins, and both are preserved* (Matthew 9:17).

In ancient times, the wine bottles were made of goat or oxen skins to protect the wine. So, what Jesus was saying is an old wineskin eventually becomes tender and easily ruptured, and when you put new wine into the old wineskin, it ferments, swells, and bursts open. However, the new skins would yield to the fermenting wine and be strong enough to hold it from bursting.

A wineskin is a government based on relationships establishes kingdom realities on the earth. It is a spiritual order that is organic, familial, and connected by covenant commitment and love for Christ and each other. A wineskin helps provide an articulated flow of communication throughout the body. I see the wineskin as the veins running through the body that carries the blood because when communication stops flowing to a part of the body, that part of the body starts to die until the blockage is addressed.

A wineskin is the defined, articulated, and the communicated values that keep us on the mission and for the right reason. A kingdom wineskin must always be relational because the kingdom of God is not composed of ideologies, theories, and disciplines, but rather the knitting together of supernatural relationships.

WE STOP HEARING WHEN WE STOP LISTENING

Sometimes, I hear people say they don't hear God's voice, and then I notice something, when I try talking with them, they are not listening. It's not that they don't hear God; it's that they don't hear anybody. I am a little worried because it seems like humanity lost its ability to communicate. Richard Nordquist, who holds a Ph.D. in Rhetoric and English at the University of Georgia, expanded the definition of communication to mean, "Communication is the process of sending and receiving messages through verbal or nonverbal means, including speech, or oral communication; writing and graphical representations (such as infographics, maps, and charts); and signs, signals, and behavior. More simply, communication is said to be "the creation and exchange of meaning."[7] Communication involves two groups, the sender and the receiver, and each has unique responsibilities to ensure effective communication.

"Because communication involves at least two distinct individuals and these individuals bring their biases into any conversation, the cause of any miscommunication can be on either the sender or the receiver end. Understanding the responsibilities of each participant can help us understand the causes of communication failure and how to prevent it."[8]

As noted, speaking is only fifty percent of communication. Imagine if you had a cell phone that could send the message, but there was no ability to respond. Or on the contrary, suppose you are at a stadium concert, and the band begins to play, but there are no outdoor speakers. This a picture of the modern human experience and the communication breakdown. A generation is adorning the earth and wants to be seen but not see, wants to be heard but has no time or patience to listen.

If we were to meet once a week for coffee, and you demonstrated you were incapable of hearing, and all you wanted to do was speak, I would probably talk less and less because of the apparent indication that you do not value what I have to share. At some point, if you did not respond appropriately to my direct, kind, and affectionate rebuke, I would stop meeting with you.

If you desire to carve out a revival realm, you must learn the art of listening. Unfortunately, most people's concept of prayer is a one-way conversation, speaking without taking the time to listen for God's response. If you think prayer looks like verbal diarrhea, you will absolutely miss out on what He wants to say to you. One of the most important aspects of representing the Lord and creating revival realms on the earth is listening to the Lord whenever He wants to speak. It is not a question of whether or not God is speaking, the question is, are we listening?

COMMUNICATION WITH YOUR SPOUSE

Recently, I was on a ministry trip where I toured several churches within three regions over a week. As we went from church to church, I noticed that many of the pastors who were leading revival cultures were doing so at the expense of neglecting their wives and families. In a couple of the churches, the pastor's wives refused to go to church, and in one particular case, the pastor's children and spouse had backslidden. His response was, "That is the cost of revival."

The truth was, he was making irresponsible choices without listening to anybody. He became addicted to the adrenaline associated with hosting renewal meetings that he was willingly handing his family over to the enemy.

I've seen some men get way too excited about placing their wives and children on the altar for the sake of "revival." This is a sad occurrence. God is not the one asking them to sacrifice their family for the sake of good meetings. God is asking them to lay down their lives, not for revival, but for their bride. In Ephesians 5:25, Paul emphasizes the priority of loving the wife sacrificially. "Husbands, love your wives, as Christ loved the church and gave himself up for her."

We must never create a martyr complex in the name of revival. When people believe they are victims because they choose to follow the Spirit's moving, they stop hearing and listening. A victim mentality will push you to a radically dangerous narcistic trajectory. When you mix a messianic complex with narcissism, victim mentality and revival meetings, you will end up with one heck of a mess.

Sometimes, when joking with the leadership team at Seattle Revival Center, I'll say, "The Lord has spoken, and Andrea told me 'no.'" People laugh because it's funny, but I'm not entirely joking.

One primary way God speaks to me, warns me, and leads me, is through my wife. Our spouses see and hear things we cannot. It is not a threat to my leadership and masculinity; it complements and protects it. When a husband and wife are not in unity and yet they persist in their ministry work, their disunity will pollute the atmosphere. You can usually discern disunity as confusion. Sadly, many ministers blame the atmosphere on the people instead of taking responsibility for their own issues that are affecting the environment.

If we carve out revival realms with hopes of sustainability, we must covenant together to honor, involve, and protect our spouses and families. Ministers who dishonor their spouse should not be trusted with the body of Christ. You cannot tell me you love and honor the church if you do not actively love your spouse. The red flags of unhealthy ministerial marriages have been ignored long enough. Revival is not the destination; it is the portal. We are on a journey to actualize and manifest healthy and intimate union.

COMMUNICATION WITH YOUR FRIENDS

In 2015, our church withdrew from the Assemblies of God. As a leadership team, we heard from the Lord, and over the course of a year, we gracefully made the transition to become a non-denominational church. It is not that we were anti-denomination. Not at all. But when we searched the fabric of kingdom networks, fellowships, and denominations, we did not find one with our DNA. One of the questions people continued asking was regarding covering and accountability for the church. It was interesting how people equated denominational affiliation with covering. It was like if you are with a denomination, then you are obviously accountable. I often explained that the kingdom of God is composed of relational alignments, and I believe the best accountability stems from a loving relationship. I would then explain how our church is aligned relationally with leaders, churches, and movements locally, regionally, nationally, and globally.

God speaks to us, inspires us, and corrects us through institutional, traditional, or intimate forms of accountability, but the quality of relationships within determines these wineskins' effectiveness. If you are a part of a church, but there is a lack of fellowship, you will have difficulty hearing because there's not a lot of speaking, let alone honest, heart-to-heart connection.

We need friends who will tell us the truth and friends to whom we listen. If you don't have any friends, there may be a reason for that absence. There's plenty of good books on how to make friends. The point is, we need to listen to what God is trying to say through our relationships, and we need to make up our minds that we will not attempt to initiate revival without relationships.

The first thing Jesus did when he started his ministry was to go and make disciples. The twelve disciples followed Jesus, learned from him, and tried to do whatever he said. In a way, they were his servants. But Jesus wasn't looking for servants; he was looking for friends who would become partners with him in ministry, and yet, the servant test was a prerequisite to becoming a friend.

In John 15:15 Jesus says, "*I no longer call you servants, because a servant does not know his master's business. Instead, I have called you friends, for everything that I learned from my Father I have made known to you.*"

This is important. Developing relationships is a process. Jesus wasn't willing to call them friends starting on day one. There had to be a foundation of trust built and instilling agreed-upon values. This verse is intuitive and radical because Jesus is saying, "Look guys, I trust you, and now you get to know my Father's secrets."

Do you want to be like Jesus? If so, then don't surround yourself with employees and servants. Make disciples, build trust, and then promote them to the friendship level. Friendship is a key to ministry longevity. Leadership and ministry can be lonely and depressing, or they can be exhilarating and exciting. Include others, and do not forget to listen.

LEARN TO LISTEN TO YOURSELF

You are a tripartite being with a body, soul, and spirit, and one of your tripartite being may try to communicate with you. In today's culture, burnout and fatigue are becoming commonplace. Friends and family members often feel helpless watching people they love while they blow out their adrenal glands. Many leaders are so good at being in "the zone" that no matter how dead they are internally they can consistently execute an A+ game externally. I love the cloud of witnesses, and yet I would rather enjoy life here and now with you than have the saints cheering me on from the cloud. We must not accidentally commit suicide by trying to open a revival portal. One of the main ways the Lord speaks to us is through our body, and for this reason, it is essential we honor and listens to what our body is trying to say.

Many of us listen to our bodies the way a mother ignores a whiny three-year-old while trying to fold some clothes. We hear something agitating, but we do not take the time to focus on what is being said. We must learn to listen to our bodies the same way a doctor will listen. Doctors listen with all of their senses. A doctor knows that a diligent and thoughtful examination determines the care of their patient. It is time that we take responsibility for our bodies.

1 Corinthians 6:19-20, the author reminds us that our bodies are temples of the Holy Spirit. In Ephesians 5:28, men are instructed to love their wives like they love their own bodies.

As sons and daughters of God, we should be our primary care physicians, and our doctors should be our secondary care physicians. We should care for and listen to what the Lord is saying through our bodies, and we should recognize that healthy bodies are a reflection of the body of Christ and the health of our ministry.

I have seen a direct correlation between my health and the health of the community I pastor. The Lord often challenges me regarding my health, and when I apply discipline and meet the objectives, there is a correlating spiritual shift that takes place within the church.

If we carve out a healthy revival realm, then we need to listen to our body and the body of Christ. There are needs within the body, and as sons and daughters of God who have been given authority within the community, and body ministry, we can be sure we are healthy and vibrant, no matter what the season.

HE WHO HAS AN EAR, LET HIM HEAR

We should not assume we will start listening to the Lord when He starts moving to the degree that we would like Him to move. Start listening and obeying Jesus today.

HERE ARE SOME QUESTIONS FOR YOU:

1. What has Jesus been trying to tell you through your friends and family?

_____

_____

_____

2. What has Jesus been trying to tell you through your spouse?

_____

_____

_____

3. What has Jesus been trying to tell you at Church?

_____

_____

_____

. . .

4. What has Jesus been trying to tell you through the Bible?

_____

_____

_____

5. What has Jesus been trying to tell you through your body?

_____

_____

_____

CHAPTER FIVE

COLLABORATION

"When I was a kid, there was no collaboration; it's you with a camera bossing your friends around. But as an adult, filmmaking is all about appreciating the talents of the people you surround yourself with and knowing you could never have made any of these films by yourself."
—Steven Spielberg

KINGDOM CREATION REQUIRES COLLABORATION

HAVE YOU EVER had difficulty stewarding your destiny? Have you found it impossible to get traction in the area of ministry and kingdom opportunities? Perhaps this has caused you to isolate, and hide your dreams, goals, and desires from others.

Sometimes, we resemble the likeness of a snail, protected underneath its shell, as we slowly shuffle through life, hoping nobody will notice us. Sometimes, when we have unique ideas, unfortunately, some attempt to bury the idea. Something inside the human psyche often pulls us in an adverse direction deceiving us with words like these, "If it's worth doing, it's worth doing it alone. That way, if you fail, no one will ever know." An unwillingness to be accountable is associated with protecting the project, which can cost the world extensively. Isolation is a critical factor that prohibits the vision from manifesting. Great creations do not necessarily demand collaboration, but self-sustaining kingdom endeavors require nothing less than collaboration.

One of the enemy's tactics is to convince people that community and collaboration will cost them the integrity of their vision. I have seen countless dreams die in isolation. I have experienced the thrill of the launch, and the disappointment of a premature landing, not because I lacked passion, but because I lacked the structure required for sustainability and never sought counsel and collaborated with others.

You were created in the image and likeness of a brilliant Creator who chose to shape the symphony of Heaven and Earth within the context of a community and collaboration. Genesis 1:26 says, ",*Then God said, 'Let __us__ make man in __our__ image, after __our__ likeness. And let them have dominion over the fish of the sea and over the birds of the heavens and over the livestock and over all the earth and over every creeping thing that creeps on the earth.'"*

This text declares that if it's worth doing, it's worth doing together. I believe there is creativity that can only be exercised within the context of community. The best thing I am creating now is because I created it with my friends.

Do not become revival dictators, shaking your fist at worship leaders, ministers, and people, just because the environment or outcome doesn't align with your preferences. The Charismatic circuit has a history of Lone Ranger Revivalists who were so hot and bright that they ended up burning down every bridge they ever built. The purpose of being a burning one isn't to be a childish arsonist. There is a better way.

WE ARE A BODY

"For as in one body we have many members, and the members do not all have the same function, so we, though many, are one body in Christ, and individually members one of another. Having gifts that differ according to the grace given to us, let us use them: if prophecy, in proportion to our faith; if service, in our serving; the one who teaches, in his teaching; [8] the one who exhorts, in his exhortation; the one who contributes, in generosity; the one who leads, with zeal; the one who does acts of mercy, with cheerfulness" (Romans 12:4-8).

Paul's writing highlights the necessity of partnership, collaboration, and synchronization within the church. He accomplished this by comparing the church to the human body. In doing so, he created a new innovative schematic for pioneering tribes and developing their organizations. In the West, corporations tend to be modeled like machines; a complicated system of cogs and sprockets linked together, but humans are not like a machine, and leadership should understand this truth. We are not composed of metal and screws, and our cells and systems are complex, nor are they easily replaceable. Our bodies function by a complicated collaboration of unique quantum systems that are subconsciously organized and held together in perfect unity by the relationship between our head and the heart.

Modern-day organizations are becoming less institutional and more organic. As of February 1st, 2018, Amazon boasted of employing more than five hundred and sixty-six thousand people! The old hierarchy-based business model could not sustain such an organization. Unfortunately, the church tends to shift from scarcely operational to systematically operational. Meanwhile, marketplace pioneers change their operations mindsets from working as mere organizations to thriving enterprises and multiplying like a living organism. Mutual interdependence is replacing the independent spirit business model. The trust factor is emerging as the foundation by which commerce is achieving unprecedented returns. The biblical values of communication and community-creation are the vehicles by which innovation cultures take businesses farther and faster into groundbreaking models, quicker than any solo entrepreneur could ever engineer.

To effectively carve out a revival realm, you cannot think small and individualistic. You must be a forward-thinker and initiate a collaborative ecosystem that moves from innovation to transformation. It would be best if you thought corporate. The kingdom of God is more significant than race, revival style, worship preferences, local church, and it is even bigger than America.

If you are to be part of what the Father is doing, you must let down our walls and begin trusting others.

In human history, never has the world been so accessible. It is a time of technological revolution for the church, and we are in a revelation awakening. The only thing preventing the knowledge of the glory of God from covering the face of this earth is the Bride of Christ continuing as isolated introverts. If we disappear as individuals, and hide our gospel-centered communities, surely this dim flame will be invisible for cities and nations. We live in a revelation revolution, and we must not let this window of opportunity dissipate. **Closed Off for Collaboration** In September 2018, I was with Anthony Rivisto, one of my best friends and closest partners in ministry.

We were dreaming, strategizing, and discussing the future of the Seattle Revival Center. In three months, we organized our administration framework by, introducing a new prototype for our weekly staff meetings including more team members, and centered our production on trust and relationship. Anthony told me the truth, ask big questions, and gently disable the incomplete and untimely ideas I tried to propose. Also, Anthony appropriately suggested and strengthened other ideas where success became a possibility, and my relationship with Anthony revived my passion for pastoring.

Some readers may find themselves saying, "I need an Anthony in my life. What is his gift-mix? I wonder if Anthony would quit SRC and join my leadership team?" The answer is no. He's not for sale, as I smile.

For clarification, I am not talking about five-fold-ministry, DISC personality profiles (dominance, influence, steadiness, and conscientiousness), or Strength Finders. I am referring to trust, that special sauce created when we willingly open our hearts to others. When you begin to trust each other and genuinely submit your ideas, dreams, and opinions to critique, comments, and questions of others, then a divine synergy manifests, and new portals open in the Spirit.

David referenced it in Psalm 133:1-4. *Behold, how good and pleasant it is when brothers dwell in unity!* ² *It is like the precious oil on the head, running down on the beard, on the beard of Aaron, running down on the collar of his robes! It is like the dew of Hermon, which falls on the mountains of Zion! For there the* LORD *has commanded the blessing, life forevermore.*

This supernatural collaboration did not happen overnight; it took Anthony and me about two years of working together before we finally started to *really work together*, and that was not Anthony's fault. Transitions are expected, and without realizing it, I had engineered my life so people could transition in and out of my life without interfering with my momentum.

I lean toward being an independent leader, and I had difficulty knowing how to let people get close enough to see how I think. To be honest, my schedule in 2016 and 2017 was so intense that I did not allow myself extra bandwidth for relationships.

Anthony was a competent leader, and I empowered him to manage, but his heart desired to lead. For that to happen, it required trusting him and letting him into my life in a more profound way. In the Fall of 2018, Anthony dared to start speaking to me about the reality of our church-culture and vision. His insight, passion, and ideas deserved respect, and his consistency of character warranted a key to my heart. So, I let him in.

The results were incredible. For the first time in a long time, I was dreaming again. The shared details, renewed system, and potential mattered because I was no longer dreaming alone. Collaboration ignited a new passion within me. Not only that, but it also opened my love bandwidth. I could see where my heart was closed to others in the past. I could admit the mistakes I had made, and I finally saw how introverted I was.

True collaboration requires a freakish amount of trust.

Taking what is essential to you, like your vision for the future, and allowing people to share their thoughts is not comfortable. Even if it feels like people are criticizing, the leader must remain flexible. Though it is hard, it is incredibly rewarding. I have done good things, but there was a potential for greater things if I had genuinely let others run with me.

RETREAT

At the end of 2015, the Lord spoke to me and said, "You are doing local church well, but I have called you to be a revival center." We began 2016 by retreating as an elder board. Our objective was to communicate and collaborate to reach an agreement and perhaps a new revival blueprint for our community. Within two months, the plans we made were basically thrown out the window as the Apple Wine Awakening acceleration thrust us into warp speed. However, the time we invested sharing, dreaming, and connecting, were the ingredients necessary to extend a three-day conference into five weeks of extended meetings and two years of almost continuous revival meetings.

If you choose to carve out a revival wineskin, you need environments to connect and collaborate. For this reason, retreats have become a part of our wineskin. Retreats come in all shapes and sizes, but the key to a successful retreat is, yes, you guessed it, communication and collaboration. We connect and collaborate so we can successfully connect and collaborate.

DO NOT BE BLINDED BY THE BLESSING

In April of 2009, I was installed as lead pastor at Seattle Revival Center. But in 2010, our board of elders discovered an accounting oversight that put us in a significant deficit at the end of the year. At this point, we did not have the reserves to make the difference. With the uncertainty associated with the transition, we all agreed that this problem would require immediate action. Part of our recovery strategy involved cutbacks in salaries and fewer hours for our staff. It was fitting we communicated the situation to the church, informing them of the problem and our plan of action. We didn't ask the body to give more. Instead, we thanked them for their generosity, we blessed them, and we invited them to share in the problem. Together, we sought the Lord for the wisdom needed to navigate through the financial crisis.

We also used this crisis as an opportunity to evaluate our finances. A friend of mine who is an accountant and conducts audits of massive 501C3s reviewed our financial statements and records and made a list of recommendations.

With wisdom, sacrifice, and communication, the Lord intervened and exceeded our expectations for the budget that year by spending a lot less than the money coming in. There was no looking back. That is just one testimony of opportunity birthed out of the crisis. Now let's look at a crisis that came out of blessing.

In our region, several leaders gathered to discuss what revival would look like in the Northwest. They all agreed that if pastors embraced genuine unity, it would be a key to unlocking unprecedented blessings within the church. The leaders formed an organization where kingdom-minded businessmen would partner with pastors to create diverse environments, including retreats, where pastors of various streams would hang out, build relationships, and pray and dream together. Guess what happened? Because of their unity, God released a commanded blessing as mentioned in Psalms 133. *Behold, how good and how pleasant it is for brothers to live together in unity... For there the LORD commanded the blessing there* (Psalm 133:1, 3, NASB). One city opened the doors to the organization, including their public schools, and established an unprecedented relationship was between the city and the church.

The blessing required administration, leadership, oversight, and human resources. Sadly, the involvement of the business leaders and pastors slowly became a means to an end. The gatherings were no longer about creating and sustaining kingdom relationships and collaboration opportunities but felt like resource gathering events. The vision and organization that were formed to connect leaders for unity and revival died within a few months of the blessing, and a new nonprofit formed around the opportunity to serve the city, but at perhaps at the cost of regional unity.

I am not a poverty guy, but sometimes, there's nothing better for your ministry environments, creativity, and spirituality than experiencing insufficiency. During times of lack, you are forced to cut back, be creative, pray, and seek answers that can only find in community. Nations experiencing a crisis are usually the nations that encounter revival. I am not suggesting we should seek crisis. I suggest we view crisis differently.

Many assume that learning from tragedies is inevitable and automatic, but it is not. I have been pastoring long enough to see how tragedies can become patterns. We must learn *how* to educate ourselves from past mistakes and crises lest we end up wasting precious years circling around the same mountain.

Do we need a divine disruption before we intentionally engage with wisdom, communication, prayer, and collaboration? No, not necessarily. If you allow for a holy dissatisfaction to drive you into becoming your own disrupter, then you might enter into the kind of opportunities that would typically not be accessible outside of a crisis.

THE SPIRIT OF TRUTH

It is impossible to carve out a revival realm without developing a relational culture that values and practices deliberate communication and collaboration. Deprived of these ingredients, the required trust needed to sustain revival will not be available. The health of our corporate gatherings is contingent on the honesty and vulnerability of the leadership culture.

The Spirit of Truth must be our ally. Communication and collaboration without honesty is a waste of time. We must guard our hearts against engaging in any form of kingdom building that involves partnering with a political spirit or censoring truth to get our way.

If leaders desire to establish a valuable work, they must be people of conviction who have clearly defined their objectives, beliefs, and values. As we covenant to create healthy environments where communication and collaboration can occur without being forced, then I believe we will see more kingdom hubs on the earth reflecting an organic and beautiful connection with Holy Spirit and the people, both inside and outside the church.

If you want to carve out your unique expression of revival that is both sustainable and integrous, you will want to be able to clearly articulate your relational convictions and expectations. Once they are clearly defined, be resolved, and willing to fight for them.

This must be our commitment: "We refuse to do revival and kingdom outside of healthy relationships."

CHAPTER SIX

CELEBRATION

*"The more you praise and celebrate your life,
the more there is in life to celebrate."*[10]
—Oprah Winfrey

CELEBRATING IS ONE of the most critical and yet neglected values needed in carving out a revival realm. We must find frequent opportunities to cease from activity to acknowledge success and honor the people that made it possible. When a football team wins a game, they celebrate their victory, including coaches, the teamwork, and all the factors that made the victory possible. Can you imagine trying to remove the celebratory aspects from football? That would be unacceptable. Yet, somehow, someone eliminated it in the church. Someone siphoned the fun out of fundamentalism. I love how John Crowder worded it, "Jesus turned the water into wine, and the church has been trying to turn it back into water ever since."

The gospel does not mean good news for all humanity once the world is rid of evil. The gospel means good news, period. Jesus conquered evil! Now, let's assimilate the realities of this victory into the earthly realm.

THE BIG FAT LIE OF RELIGION

Today's culture works overtime, convincing us we are not happy. You might think you're happy, but you are not. Do you want to know why? Because you are hungry.

In 2010, it was reported that 4.6 billion dollars were spent by the American fast-food industry alone only to inform us that we're not happy yet. Because we are hungry, we will not be satisfied until we eat a buttery bacon cheeseburger with extra bacon. Billboard signs, radio commercials, and television ads do not work for those who recently ate. It exists for those who forgot to eat and are now starving for a juicy flame-broiled patty.

Today's marketing culture creates systems that ensure our deficits and forever torment us. Where do these obsessions lead us? It leads us to a negative portal into the non-relenting rat race with its perpetual prodding to crush it, work harder, and a sleep-less-mentality. Advertising dollars continue to remind us that more possessions justify the pain, exhaustion, and poor health required to succeed. The reality is many believed this lie, "We are only as relevant as our mobile device is current."

To a great degree, the church lost her joy. Not all at once, and not completely, but slowly and surely, the enemy tricked the church into thinking Jesus doesn't satisfy. Many charismatic Christians believe the Holy Spirit comes and goes. Our desperation songs and pleading prayers became a new theology that I call twiggy theology, a skin-and-bones form of Christianity that needs to be confronted. Too many church leaders are burning out, and too many pastors are making unwise choices because the grind of joyless religion has imprisoned them.

Religion says, "You cannot celebrate yourself because you have not done enough." The Gospel says, "You are worthy to be celebrated, because you are in Christ, and He is worthy to be celebrated."

Religion says, "You cannot celebrate what God is doing in your home group, church, job, or in your family. It's not BIG enough!"

The Gospel says, "You are a child of God, and every small accomplishment is worth celebrating."

There is no such thing as a religious spirit. It is a demon, a big fat bully that torments people. It's time to punch that sucker in the nose and throw a party.

BAD PROGRAMMING

In 1 Corinthians 3:19, Paul rebukes the believers for ascribing to worldly wisdom, which Paul said was foolishness (interpreted as mental dullness). The word "worldly" in Greek is cosmos. He is saying, "You think that wisdom is a human endeavor, a collection of lessons accumulated from other's timelines, but real wisdom is spiritual and comes from the Holy Spirit."

We don't have an appropriate number of celebrations in the church because we have allowed cosmic wisdom to define when it is appropriate to celebrate.

Paul addresses bad programming in Romans 12:2 by commanding the believers with these piercing words, *"Do not be conformed to this world, but be transformed by the renewal of your mind, that by testing you may discern what is the will of God, what is good and acceptable and perfect."*

Paul says we must not put on the world's electromagnetic brain-washing helmet that tricks us into seeing the world through vanity lenses of covetousness, and jealousy. When we submit to the *keeping-up-with-the-Joneses-mentality,* we opt out of Father's business, and soon discover we no longer have the bandwidth for kingdom activity because we swallowed the brown pill of Western commercialism that leads to consumerism.

Here's an unfortunate truth: the world doesn't care if you die. They will mourn your loss for twenty-four hours, and then another hamster will replace you. Why would you kill yourself running after the dangling carrot? In this ridiculous maze, enough is never enough.

With every success, there is a bundle of new challenges. In

this system, we designate most of our emotional fuel towards our careers while our family is left with the fumes. From what my father-in-law tells me, "Nobody ever grows old and says, 'I wish I would have worked more.'"

A deficiency-based obsession convinces us we should be afraid because we do not, nor will we ever have enough. The dearth lie is quite convincing and is one of the biggest factors for why Christians have difficulty regularly celebrating Jesus and others. Perhaps we think that celebration is premature.

It's time to pull the stainless-steel umbilical cord in the back of our necks and unplug from the matrix inside the artificial world that enslaves and exploits us with its worldly data. We have been lied to and given a bogus script. It's time to break it and then break it again.

CELEBRATION IS THE KEY

My good friend Christ White once asked me an interesting question, "Do you know why envy is a sin?" I was a pastor, so obviously, I knew the answer, but I wanted to see if he knew. I asked curiously, "Why Chris?" He responded, "Because," continuing in a very confident teacher-tone, "when we are envious for what we don't have, we are saying, 'God, what you blessed me with, isn't enough.'" *"Wow,"* I thought to myself, *"I didn't think I knew that."* But I didn't tell him that, of course.

Matching your well-dressed, super-car-driving neighbor cannot be your motivation. It's time to abandon the worldly drive and realize that celebration is the key to entering into His courts.

To carve out a revival realm, we must exit off the road leading to the American-dream and denominationalism treadmill and start realigning our priorities. The integrity, purity, and longevity of a move of God require we cut ties with pride, jealousy, envy, and greed. Our excuses to not celebrate Jesus are deceptive lies that detain us in a subconscious poverty spirit. Stop striving for what you already have.

Trust me. You have enough. Now is an appropriate time to celebrate Jesus!

TOO RIGHTEOUS TO PARTY

In the parable of the prodigal son, the older brother refused to enter his father's party because of jealousy. Believing he was the one deserving to be celebrated, he considered his father reckless in celebrating a disgraceful son who deserved to be punished.

How did the father respond to his older son? He *reminds* him with these words, "You are my son, and everything I have is yours."

A celebration culture triggers any un-regenerated orphan spirit that may be lording it over our thoughts. When jealousy keeps us out of the party, we need to be reminded, "We are celebrated sons too!" The spirit of religion wants to kill a celebration culture and enforce its anti-keep working spirit.

CELEBRATE, IT IS UNDERWEAR DAY

Every calendar is separated into seasons, and each season has its appointed culturally accepted moments of celebration. Did you read culturally accepted moments? What are you thinking? Can you imagine telling your boss that you wouldn't be showing up to work on Monday because you and your family will be celebrating Underwear Day? That might get you to laugh and then fired.

Sure, underwear deserves to be celebrated; it is one of the most brilliant and underappreciated creations. Where would we be without underwear? Can you imagine? I know denim would not be as popular.

However, if you showed up at work on Christmas Day, and your place of employment is closed, you use your key card to break into the office, and you chose to work anyway. Your boss would probably think you were crazy because Christmas is a recognized day of celebration and rest. Your company decided that working on that day is not an option.

It is sort of what it is like in the church. God has done so much in our lives, and He continues to be generous in His faithfulness, love, and affection, and yet, rather than creating moments of rest and celebration, we continue to work, sweat, and strive. Hi Ho, Hi Ho, it's off to work we go!! The church is like the employee who broke into the office on Christmas Day, and we wonder why the awakening atmosphere is so rare in our Sunday morning worship?

Mission, vision, and values are wonderful if they provide opportunities to give thanks to the Lord for His abundant goodness. Still, I have seen examples where organizations created high-performance environments without integrating a culture of celebration. They ended being abusive and more cultish, which is more like a sweatshop than a heavenly environment.

When it's Christmas Day, get out of the cubical and go home to your family. Learning to acknowledge and celebrate the presence of God is not a luxury but a necessity in preparing, stewarding, and sustaining a move of God.

Give thanks to the Lord because every day is underwear day!

SCHEDULE TIME TO CELEBRATE

A celebration should not be random any more than birthdays are random. Celebrations should be consistent, memorable, and repeatable. Our patterns of celebration should establish a celebratory precedent. In Leviticus 23:3, the Lord gave the children of Israel a twelve-month rhythm of rest with celebrations. Seven feasts or celebrations were literally commanded as consecrated times. These moments served as milestones throughout the year. They were scheduled moments of reflection, sacrifice, and celebration. This wasn't just a fun and silly time when you could slack off and not work; these celebrations had significant value in God's eyes. Declining to celebrate Yahweh's command when scheduled, it would be viewed as a disgraceful and dishonoring act, worthy of judgment and even death.

PARTNERS

In the Father's business, we are not employees; we are partners. As we partner with the Father and begin to see the justice and righteousness of the kingdom of heaven penetrate our reality, these manifestations deserve honor, a special honor called celebration.

When we choose to celebrate what the Father is doing in our families, relationships, teams, businesses, and churches, what we are saying is, "Everybody stop working. Halt your production. Turn your attention to the grace of God that has actualized in our midst. Let us do something different that is drastic and let us create a memory stone at this very moment!" Jesus gave us plenty of excuses to celebrate Him. The only appropriate response right now is to rejoice and join the heavenly party!"

The church seems to think that the sound of revival resembles desperation and hunger, including young people at the altar, who are sweating, screaming, and crying. As important as that sounds, there is a particular revival sound that resembles the story of the Prodigal Son and the party his dad orchestrated for him. Moves of God are sustained through deliberate celebration by taking the time to intentionally honor the accomplishments and the abiding presence of the Lord. What is the sound of revival? It sounds like rejoicing and celebration.

A serious paradigm shift is currently needed. Our twisted consciousness needs to get flipped like a burning pancake. The "we still do not have enough' and the 'God you have to do something" mentality needs to transition to a "let's stop multitasking and let's stinkin' party!" Our lives should include the sabbath rest, a daily celebration when we rejoice in God's grace with specificity and unity.

. . .

BIG BUTS
PERSONAL APPLICATION

Celebration begins with a choice. Even now, you can choose the joy of grace or choose to defer hope and wait until we finally enter our mythical promise land. If the land flowing with milk and honey is anything but Christ, we are putting our faith in fantasy versus the reality of Christ. The most important word mentioned above is "choose." Joy is a choice. When we stop delaying joy, we can shift our focus away from future gifts to present graces. Trust me, there is plenty of evidence demonstrating God's grace in your life, and if you don't see them, then you are not looking.

I'm not saying your life doesn't suck. Maybe it does, and if so, I'm sorry. But I will say this with love and a sincere smile on my face. "Stop feeling sorry for yourself." Life is too short to sulk your life away in a dreary bathtub of despair. Today, choose to cut through the disappointment and begin carving a new reality. I am not saying it will not be easy, but I am saying it is possible.

Nobody models this transition better than King David. There are more laments in the Psalms than any other genre of songs. The book of Psalms reminds us of a country- western song about broken hearts and missed opportunities. But guess what, in almost every lament, there is a perception shift, a Pattern Interrupt. David cuts through the facts until he finds the timeless and absolute truths. There is usually a moment when David says, "but," and it is always one big 'but.' But God is my helper (Psalm 54:4).

Big 'buts' change the scene. It is the word you see when the camera pans away from the obstacle towards the heavens. Go ahead, recount the facts that justify grumbling and complaining, and now insert a big "but" afterward. But what? You need to start stating facts about who God is by looking at what the Lord has done. Congratulations, you just shifted your laments to a praise song. If you want to carve out a revival realm where you see God hijack your faculties to release His supernatural glory, then you can't allow yourself to be discouraged by the past or even the present. You need to insert a giant 'but' into the equation and begin to celebrate the One whose life, love, and sacrifice have changed your possibilities forever.

As you intentionally celebrate Jesus, faith in God increases in your life. People often come to me with big, serious problems, and there is a big faith-filled "Awesome!" that slips out. Celebrating Jesus creates a faith-filled excitement in the room that results in supernatural faith with new and radical confidence in God's ability and wiliness to show up and shift the problem into an opportunity. You can't control outcomes, but you can control moments. You have the authority and ability to change the atmosphere from grief to glory. The results are in the Lord's hands; the atmospheres are in ours.

PARTY HOUSE
FAMILY APPLICATION

The place to begin carving out realms of revival is in our homes. The family is a micro-city and contains nation-changing and generational-shaping influence. It is the role of a mommy and daddy to shape the family, but not the school system's role or the local church. The fathers and mothers are the apostolic and prophetic platform by which the house is built. If we believe this to be true, we can shape these values into our family culture, and the surrounding culture will change as a result.

I would encourage you to adopt a culture of celebration in your home. Begin by committing to raise children in a household who believe that thanksgiving and celebration are a normal part of daily life.

Find creative ways to celebrate each other. Create opportunities to party together as a family. Design fun and playful awards, host award ceremonies, and publicly honor the family members for their character, achievements, and most importantly, for taking bold risks.

Figure out how to revive religious traditions such as praying for the food and before bed reading the Bible together. Last but not least, make a calendar of your celebrations. At the beginning of each year, schedule your weekly and monthly family activities and celebrations. For example, make every Monday night a time for family communion before bed. Consider every weeknight for a time to read a Bible story from the children's adventure Bible. If it's not on the calendar, it's not a priority. Get religious about your celebrations and begin carving out a new revival realm in your home.

PARTY HOUSE
CHURCH APPLICATION

Not a church leader? That's okay—volunteer to host a party. Host a party at the church or at your home. Find a group of people in your church who are typically overlooked and celebrate them. Not only that but share the celebration on your social media platform. Tell the story and invite others to begin honoring the forgotten.

Are you a church leader? That's okay too. Celebrate everybody. Celebrate your visitors, celebrate the people who have been in your church forever, celebrate your staff and volunteers, and celebrate the people in your community who refuse to go to your church. At the Seattle Revival Center, we host an annual Christmas party to celebrate our volunteers, staff, and elders. The party reaches almost three hundred people, and we go all out to participate. It is almost offensive how much money we spend celebrating the people who gave their time, passion, energy, and leadership all year long. At the party, we announce all the victories, and we celebrate Jesus for the evidence of God's grace. We use the party as an opportunity to cast a vision for the upcoming year. Our Christmas church party is one of our favorite annual traditions.

I chat with pastors and church leaders all the time who are discouraged about the size of their church or the lack of momentum. I share with them that celebration is an incredible pattern interrupt.

Church leaders, the worst thing we can ever do is create a culture of criticism and accusation in our worship environments. Pessimism is worse than herpes. Sometimes, what happens is we blame our people for the areas where we feel powerless. Let's be honest for a second. It is not uncommon to feel powerless, but instead of playing the blame game, we need to interrupt the game and start processing the facts while praising the Lord.

Sad? Celebrate Jesus.

Mad? Celebrate Jesus.

Rad? Bahahaha. Celebrate Jesus.

And don't just celebrate. Be creative and create celebrations.

MY FIRST DECADE

Slowly, I began waking up, while smacking my lips together and groaning. My thirty-seven-year-old body felt the revenge of gravity. My right arm lurked over the right side of my face covering my eyeball that was, you guessed it, sore, really sore. I groaned with creation. I knew what it was. It happened before. A stye was developing. I hate styes. A stye is painful and invisible until it gets more visible, and even more visible until you finally look like you ran into an angry and possibly drunk Mike Tyson in a dark alley. For a preacher, who wrestles with maybe just a little bit of vanity, I stinkin' hate styes with a passionate and perfect hatred. After looking in the mirror, I immediately thought, "Anthony will have to preach tomorrow."

I sent Anthony a text, "Yo, I need you to preach tomorrow; I got a stye in my right eye." Anthony hit me back with, "You serious?" Of course, I was serious. Who would kid about having a stye? Anthony seemed weird about it, but he agreed.

That night, about five-thirty people arrived at our house. As they were eating, I and my painful eye was thinking like, "What is going on?" The elders of our church were throwing a surprise party to honor me for ten years of pastoral ministry.

It was an amazing unforgettable night, but at the end of the celebration, one of our elders (Sandi) came up to me and informed me that I would be attending the second service tomorrow, not to preach, but to attend. The Sandi spirit of fear came upon me, so I agreed.

The next day at church, I found myself at the surprise party of the century. The church hijacked the service and created a tribute to Pastor Darren. Several people prepared speeches and a special video covering my first ten years of pastoral ministry, with the most amazing decorations and dessert, all in a Hollywood theme. I was humbled and so amazed that I didn't know how to receive such honor.

Part of living in a revival realm means we celebrate others and also learn how to be celebrated. I noticed that often the people who don't know how to receive the honor are the very people who struggle to show honor.

My church didn't just celebrate me that day. They actively loved me. They loved me with gifts, words of affirmation, hugs, and acts of service.

You see, celebration is a banner employing all the love languages. When we celebrate each other, and humble ourselves and receive celebration, we glorify God by participating in His amazing grace that made all these realities possible.

A part of me was sad that day. Then, a thought hit me. I wondered how many faithful pastors I know who have laid their lives down for the church and served much longer than me and yet, were never celebrated like I was. As I think about it now, I am thinking of some ways to celebrate some incredible people.

At the end of the day, a celebration isn't just some cheesy thing we do to feel better about ourselves and others. Celebration carries tremendous gravity because celebration pulls heaven down to earth with its tremendous value.

One day you will be celebrated. One day your heavenly Father will pick you up off the ground and twirl you around, celebrating His love for you. He will place you on His shoulders and dance in the heavenly realm declaring and singing, "Here is my child at last, in whom I am well pleased!"

How can we not give people a taste of what heaven will be like before they die?

CHAPTER SEVEN

EVALUATION

"True genius resides in the capacity for evaluation of uncertain, hazardous, and conflicting information."
—*Winston Churchill*

SHAW-FAT

THE KINGDOM OF God is composed of divine alliances and assignments. These alliances involve the commitments and investments of people, their time, and their passion. For too long, the church got away with wasting people's time, gifts, and anointings, and I don't think it is intentional. Maybe Christians were never taught how to carve out a discipline for evaluation.

According to Webster's Dictionary, evaluation is the act of evaluating something, thereby determining its value, nature, character, or quality. The Hebrew word for this concept is the word *shaphat* pronounced shaw-fat' and it means to judge.

We saved the most difficult and perhaps the most important of our six disciplines for last. They are the practice of honest, spirit-led evaluation. This value creates radical tension in the supernatural stream of Christianity because many people feel they have no control over the results in their lives. Even more dire, many supernaturalists within the church ignore attention to their lack of results. Suppose in Matthew 7:19, Jesus said that any tree that bears no fruit should be plucked up and thrown into the fire, shouldn't that mean we should evaluate our fruitfulness?

Self-evaluation is one of the least talked about subjects in the church, usually because people confuse honest assessment with condemnation. In ministry especially, fruitlessness can feel like bareness. The voice of accusation has a way of nagging a believer's identity, causing one to retreat from all sense of responsibility and commitments. For this reason, many in ministry refrain from asking the question, "Are my efforts sustainable?" An honest assessment may seem overwhelmingly negative; however, the cost of avoidance is often more than any of us can personally afford. When we fail to apply forethought into our efforts and activities, burnout becomes predictable and inevitable.

The parables of Jesus emphasize the tremendous amount of responsibility in understanding the kingdom's gravity and our willingness to be excellent stewards. For example, the parable of the talents in Matthew 25:14-30, gives attention to results and matters significantly to the Lord. If we decide to steward and sustain a move of God, we must learn what it means to carve out a culture of evaluation, where individuals are equipped and mentored to righteously judge their fruitfulness within the safety of the Father's acceptance and unwavering love.

Assume you want to carve out a realm of unprecedented fruitfulness, where the harvest is supernaturally natural and normal. In that case, you must receive empowerment to become righteous judges in our world.

In 1 Corinthians 6, the believers in Corinth are going a bit crazy. One of Paul's issues is that the believers are always in court suing each other. So, in his letter to the Corinthians, Paul sternly corrects them with these words.

When one of you has a grievance against another, does he

dare go to law before the unrighteous instead of the saints? Or do you not know that the saints will judge the world? And if the world is to be judged by you, are you incompetent to try trivial cases? Do you not know that we are to judge angels? How much more, then, matters pertaining to this life! So, if you have such cases, why do you lay them before those who have no standing in the church? I say this to your shame. Can it be that there is no one among you wise enough to settle a dispute between the brothers (1 Corinthians 6:1-5, ESV).

Paul questions their dignity, saying, "Have you no dignity, no sense of self-awareness?" Paul is concerned because the believer's immaturity is making a mocking the testimony of Jesus. The major issue here is not lawsuits, but that the church is neglecting its identity as righteous judges who are called to judge immorality and injustice. There is a reason why sandwiched between is the issue about lawsuits and the stern warning regarding sexuality immorality. What do sexuality immorality and lawsuits in the church have anything to do with each other? They exist because of a lack of righteous justice. The body of Christ is failing to take care of the people. Paul says, 'how do you expect to steward the earth and the heavens if you cannot steward your own body?'

Pastors, how can you pastor a church if you are failing to pastor your own family? Revivalists, how can you bring revival to America if your own soul is dead?

The judgments of God are always for the sake of restoring the righteous justice of God. You can be a dispenser of heavenly justice, thereby actualizing God's original intent into the present. For example, think of Adam and Eve in the garden before their disobedience created separation, because it is a glimpse of God's original intent for humanity and the earth. Our empowerment as the righteous to bring judgment enables us with the practical ability to restore fruitfulness to every area of bareness.

. . .

YOUR OLD COUCH IS UGLY

Andy Stanley, famous for lessons in leadership, addresses the need to have fresh eyes to evaluate the efficiency of our environments honestly. To prove his point, he uses the illustration of an old and ugly couch. Andy rightfully points out, "Nobody ever knows that they have an old and ugly couch."

Andy asks the question, "How many of you have ever gone to someone's house and thought, 'that is one ugly couch?'"

For the outsider, everything is new, and therefore everything is fair game for evaluation and judgment. Outsiders and newbies always see what is hideous because they don't live in the environment. Andy argues that we need to develop the stranger's perspective, and deal with the old ugly couches in our environments. In a nutshell, this involves creating a culture of evaluation.

Although it is natural to evaluate others continuously, it is ineffective. You are responsible for yourself. If you are too busy to engage with kingdom activities, that is your issue. If you have too many old couches consuming your finances, energy, and passion, maybe it's time to do an honest evaluation and eliminate some old couches.

BUT GOD GAVE ME THAT COUCH

Over time, new things become old things. If you read my book, *Pattern Interrupt*, then you know our story of a three-day conference that turned into two years of non-stop revival meetings and conferences. 2016 and 2017 were some of the most exciting years of my life. Then something happened, what was a new thing became a tradition. We were faithful in evaluating and adapting during the two year's period, but in 2018-2019, conferences became another ritual.

Each conference at SRC requires about twenty to thirty hours of time, energy, and passion for me personally. That is 360 hours per year of personal bandwidth that I devote to SRC conferences.

Not only that, but my team puts in far more hours than I do at our events. If I were to calculate the hours that our team collectively invests into conferences each year, it would be startling.

Honestly, it was a revelation to learn what was once a momentum creator at SRC had now become a significant factor for derailing our momentum. Our revival center was demanding, and my leaders wanted to serve but were over-taxed.

Every good and perfect gift comes from the Lord, but not every gift is good and perfect for every season. We are responsible to evaluate our input and output and the rate of return on our investments. In Luke 16:10, Jesus says that he who is faithful with a little will can be entrusted with much —being faithful with little means we will learn to love uncensored honesty. At times, I like the truth when I first hear it, but when I see the truth, I become accountable to take action.

Maybe God gave you a couch, and maybe it was awesome, but perhaps it is worn out now, and possibly it is wearing you out. What are the old couches you need to eliminate? Write them down in your journal. Tell a friend. Be accountable and get those old couches out of your home. They ugly.

EMBRACE THE MOVE

In February 2016, we were off like a rocket. The building was packed. Signs, wonders, miracles, salvations, deliverances, and we had no idea what we were doing. The Apple Wine Awakening continued for about two years and guess what— it did not shipwreck our church; it built the church. We are stronger, sharper, and more faith-filled today than ever. If fully embraced and properly stewarded, seasons of outpouring, will produce unprecedented fruit that brings refreshing and life-changes for families, churches, and regions.

. . .

FULLY EMBRACED

I had the honor of spending a year on the Sunshine Coast, Australia, back in the late 90s. My parents helped a church steward a mighty move of God, and I did my part by waking up every morning and surfing with my best friend. One morning we learned of some massive waves at one of our favorite beaches. We took our boogie boards because the waves were far too big for our skill level. At one point, I remember catching a wave that seemed to keep building, bigger and bigger, lifting me higher and higher. I directed the front of my board down and to the right, and the wave curled up over me. I was in the tube of the wave, and it felt like I was in a dream or at least in a real cool surfing movie. However, as I was swimming back out, instead of ducking under a giant wave, I tried to swim up and over it, but instead of going over it, it went over me. I didn't catch that wave; the wave caught me and tumbled me down into the sand. I had sand everywhere, and I mean everywhere.

There are waves of the Spirit that in the same way demand all or nothing. For example, we could look at the mighty wave of God that swept the globe in 1994 as a case study. God used South African Evangelist Rodney Howard Browne as a catalyst that awakened North America and Canada and then ignited the nations. This move of God was so disruptive that many church leaders had no idea what to do with the wave. Some churches embraced it, others rejected it, and some churches flirted with it. Catch the Fire Church in Toronto, CA, Bethel Church in Redding, CA, and Harvest Rock Church in Pasadena, CA. fully embraced the fresh wave of the Holy Spirit and quickly became revival hot spots that still impact nations to this day. Unfortunately, countless churches were also destroyed because they tried to go 50% revival.

When we don't fully commit to carving out a realm of revival, we find we cannot properly discern and assess the available opportunities. Suppose your goal is to create an atmosphere where people show up. In that case, the fear of man will be the dominant spirit by which we lead; however, if our primary objective is to create atmospheres where God shows up, then the spirit of the fear of the Lord will be the dominant spirit by which we govern.

If you are not willing to go all-in, revival will be the worst thing that ever happened to you. But, if you are willing to fully embrace, steward, and sustain the open Spirit portal, this realm of awakening will be the best thing that ever happened to not only you but your entire city.

WELCOME UNCENSORED FEEDBACK

At Seattle Revival Center, we know first-hand the importance of evaluation, and not just feedback and surveys from within our culture, but the value of seeking uncensored feedback from experienced leaders outside of it.

Every church's culture is affected by its size, and this is called a church's size culture; for the most part, this dynamic is invisible and not given much attention by most people. At Seattle Revival Center I noticed some negative elements within our size culture and my leadership capacity. I knew that changes were needed, but I didn't know what changes were critical because I never pastored a church of our size before. I didn't have a baseline for what looked normal. Our leadership team had many questions, and we needed wisdom, so we reached out to a church a few miles down the road.

We were surprised and excited when Pastor Troy Jones, pastor of New Life Church in Renton, Washington, agreed to meet us at a local restaurant. He later informed us that he had no idea who we were and thought we had scheduled the meeting to rebuke him. He was relieved to see a table with smiling youngish people waiting for him. We asked him questions for two hours, he responded with questions, we answered his questions, then left the restaurant with a new perspective worth more than gold.

Pastor Troy later came to our church to meet with our team. He asked us more questions and gave us great advice, but I could tell he had things he wanted to say. I thought maybe he was nervous about overwhelming us or hurting our feelings, and so I pulled him aside during a break and encouraged him, "Please don't sugar coat anything. We need your uncensored feedback. We can handle it."

For the rest of that meeting, he let it rip. Our familiar filters were shattered during the three hours. We saw our environment with fresh eyes. It was overwhelming and memorable.

This uncensored feedback was crucial. I needed to see a new thing, hear a new thing, and have the courage to lead our church in a fresh direction.

Proverbs 27:6 says, "Faithful are the wounds of a friend; profuse are the kisses of an enemy." As discerning and self-aware as we think we are, we need the kind of wounds that only comes from a friend.

BLAMING HELL

Over the years, I had the honor of serving countless leaders and churches. Usually, over a meal, I hear about how the church is under attack, about the warfare, and the supernatural forces that keep the church from reaching its full potential.

I know firsthand the intensity of spiritual warfare and the backlash that comes when we ride the wave of God's glorious Holy Spirit; however, most demonic attacks are against the mind. When we believe the health and growth of the body of Christ were restricted by the enemy, despite the intensity of the attack, there is a relief in knowing that the spiritual vibrancy of the church is out of our control.

When I give advice or offer suggestions, many leaders' eyes glaze over, as if they are asking themselves, "Did he not hear a word I said. It is not our fault. It's hell's fault!"

Blaming hell brings a false sense of comfort. Even though we feel better about our leadership, if we are under attack, we must be doing something right; constantly blaming Satan does not usually fix our lack of fruitlessness.

When we blame principalities and powers habitually, we unknowingly disempower the spiritual authority Jesus gave us to deal with injustice. Rather than being hyper-spiritual, sometimes we should begin by being hyper-repentant, seeking the Lord for the truth that brings freedom.

EVALUATION AND PROPHETIC WORDS

Another pothole to recognize and avoid is blaming our foolish choices on the voice of God or prophetic words. I am sure you have prophetic words on tapes and probably a plethora of prophetic words recorded on your cell phone. I sure do. There are many promises from the Lord that I still steward and cultivate. When it comes to stewarding prophetic words, I am among the most prudent in ensuring that a word does not get discarded. At Seattle Revival Center, we greatly honor and cherish the prophets and the prophetic.

The problem is that a prophetic word from the Lord is never intended to be a blindfold. Many people use the prophetic as an excuse to not deal with the realities of the present.

Imagine being Moses and making a promise to the Israelites that God would give them a gift, a land of prosperity that is flowing with milk and honey. However, year after year, imagine being Moses and having this incredible prophetic word, a promise, that the Lord has a prosperous land prepared for the Israelites. Imagine as year after year passes by and wondering, "God, when are you going to fulfill your promise?" Moses is such an incredible leader. Year after year, he holds on to the promise and selflessly leads God's people through crisis and conflict. Year after year, he puts his trust and confidence in God.

One aspect of Moses' leadership needs to focus on the tension between promise, faith, and the miraculous. Moses had a promise from the Lord, and he did not use the promise to be reckless. For example, when Moses led the Israelites through the

Red Sea, he waited for the sea to open before giving God's people the order to walk through it. Can you imagine if Moses had led the people of God into the sea before it had parted, they all would have drowned?

Sometimes, leaders think that a promise from God means that they can practice reckless faith. I have seen leaders lead their people into some of the most unfortunate circumstances imaginable, all because they thought that faith meant being radical, just to be radical. If you want to be radical in your faith, then you will want to practice radical obedience. In the kingdom, obedience triggers the miraculous, not random risk in light of an old prophetic word.

The process looks like this: we obey, the waters part, and we walk through the parted sea. If we obey and the waters don't part, then we must wait before we walk.

Sometimes we can get so outcome-driven, so promise-land focused, that we forget about the God of the journey. Something can be quite frustrating about a glorious future when you feel that the present is subpar. As I approach being forty years old, the voice of the accuser gets louder. He says, "Darren, you better work harder, work smarter, or you better figure something out. People don't care about you. You don't matter. Your work doesn't matter. Go big or go home." What is this?

This is identity exploitation. It's the act of taking someone's noble desires and shaming them because they never reached where they hoped to be within their life's timetable. I recognize this voice. It is not the voice of my Father. It is the enemy of my soul, using the desires of my soul, to get me to partner with foolishness. Satan wants me to take a "leap of faith," a leap so big I can never recover. Satan doesn't care about my marriage, my children, or my health. He wants me dead, and he wants "the ministry" to be the sword on which I fall.

The devil cannot kill me, but he can try to get me to kill myself in the name of kingdom duty. By God's grace and with the accountability of my family and friends, I endeavor to move forward, prophetically motivated and not prophetically shamed.

If you feel there is a gap between your present and your future, between the wilderness and the promise land, then be sure to guard your soul and not allow the enemy to use the gap to shame you. In the same way that the blood of Jesus liberates us from the shame of the past, his mercy in the same way can protect you in the present from being shamed by your future.

In Christ, we can confront reality. We can ignore it or become obsessed with it, but we must stand firm and honestly address where we are in the light of who we are in Christ, the sanctified desires of our hearts, and the prophetic intel we have received over the years. Your prophetic words are the beautiful tools the Lord gave you to carve. Don't neglect them.

REVIVAL BEGINS AT HOME

No matter your ministry status or level of fame and influence, we have received a level of authority so we can carve out a revival realm. Pastor Bill Johnson, a lover of revival, says, "Revival begins at home." Major historical revivals have been adverted and aborted because of bad habits that began at home. Family is the foundational paradigm framing the government for God's kingdom. A revival portal is Father's invitation to mature from thinking like an orphan to functioning as a son. The nuclear family is a prophetic drama for our spiritual family. The unity, honor, and submission demonstrated in our homes carve out a parallel realm, a corresponding reality in the kingdom. The state of our churches is a reflection of the state of our families.

In Ephesians five, Paul is basically saying, "Let's talk about marriage to get a glimpse of the corresponding reality that exists between Christ and the church." Paul directs husbands and wives about how they should conduct themselves within the home. Paul understood that marriage does not model kingdom reality; it creates kingdom reality. To carve out a revival realm within our cities, we must confront the present-day culture of our homes and families. The real question isn't whether or not there is unity in the church, but rather, is there unity, relationship, and a spirit of reconciliation within our hearts. This is why I believe this book is essential for all believers. I think we can so easily blame church leaders for the insufficiencies and defects in the church, but it's the body of Christ that must bear the image of Christ, not just leaders in the church. We are the body, and in Romans twelve, Paul says we are all vital body parts. For this reason, when Paul writes his letters to the various churches in the epistles, he writes private letters for the eyes of the leadership only. Still, also, he addresses all of the believers in the different cities to whom he writes.

Why? I'm glad you asked because revelation and evaluation are required not just for church leaders but for all believers. Our understanding and fierce commitment to align our lives with truth and model our contrasting kingdom values are what carves out a realm that can be stewarded and sustained. The generation that accepts the responsibility of stewarding His manifest presence is the generation that will experience abiding habitats of divinity – actual Jacob's ladders – modern-day Eden that begin at home and then spread to infect cities and nations.

TASTING WHAT YOU ARE COOKING

I've watched enough cooking shows to know that good cooks always taste what they cook. They evaluate, tweak, and add whatever they choose. They never trust a generic recipe or formula; they must know for themselves how the ingredients work together and blend to create flavors that carve out memories. As the people of God, we should likewise take pride in what we are creating, stewarding, and releasing. For far too long, we put the "Christian" label on everything from music, to movies, to revival meetings. We forget what Paul says in Colossians 1 that Jesus made the invisible aspects of God visible on the earth. This is our call as well. As we host Holy Spirit in our hearts, homes, businesses, and churches, we should commit to make visible the invisible realm of heaven. If it doesn't make visible the invisible Christ, it is not Christian.

What are you working on right now? What does it taste like? What should you do? Do not control these conversations with your mind. Hold them in your heart.

Take your time, and do not relent in advancing your unique opportunities assigned to you from Jesus.

CHAPTER EIGHT

THE TENSION IN TAKING ACTION

WHAT IS IT WORTH TO YOU?

I'M NOT BRAGGING about individualistic choices; I am referring to back before me. Robert Cecil Stott–my grandpa–initially gave his life to the Lord when he was seventeen years old, but soon backslid, married my grandma Rose, and took up a courier of drinking; he and his guitar loved to party. The destructive nature of trying to parent two children while being married to a person struggling with alcohol addiction became too much for my grandma to handle, so she informed him of her intent to leave him. It is within this context that my grandpa found himself at a revival meeting in Nelson, British Columbia, that his sister invited him to attend. The service had climaxed, and the minister invited those to come up to the front to identify themselves as a sinner in need of a Savior. In his heart, he declined the offer for salvation, thinking he might do it later. And that's when the Lord spoke to my grandpa and said, "It's now or never."

As the old church piano and organ began to play, my grandpa slowly raised his right hand and stood up from his pew and walked to the front of the church to surrender his life to Christ. That night, the presence of the Lord not only came upon my grandpa, but it also entered him, and began transforming him from the inside out. My grandpa would hand-roll and smoke forty cigarettes a day. When the meeting was over, he walked into the house, grabbed his stash of tobacco, rolled papers, and threw them into the fire of the kitchen stove. He then proceeded to pour out all the alcohol in his home.

My grandma was not a fan of my grandpa's conversion. I mean, what's worse than being married to a person with an alcohol disorder, except being married to a religious fanatic. But over the next few days, she studied him, and she was secretly impressed at the positive change in her husband. One night, as they laid in bed, my grandpa heard my grandma crying in bed. He leaned over to comfort her, "What is Rosie?"

She had a question for him. "What must I do to give my life to Jesus." Shortly after their conversion, Bob felt called of God to become a preacher. He sensed a passion to preach but did not have a church or a pulpit. So, he parked a huge flatbed trailer in his front yard, hooked up a loudspeaker system, and began hosting revival meetings for his neighbors, whether they liked it or not (and most of them did not).

Feeling the fire of God burning inside of him, he quit his good job and built a little chapel out of used lumber on a donated piece of land his neighbor gave him. There, in Beaver Falls, BC, he planted his first revival center. Jesus was moving, and people were getting saved, especially young people. Each week, my grandpa would preach the simple gospel everywhere he went, and as lives were transformed, the church grew.

One young man who was saved in the chapel was a boy named Larry. Each night, when he returned home from the revival meetings, his Irish Catholic father made fun of him and beat him for going to the meetings. One night, Larry's dad found the little Bible my grandma gave him and proceeded to throw the Bible into the fire. That very night a storm came, and lightning struck and burned up his dad's prized cow. Larry informed his father, "You burned my Bible. God burned your cow!" Larry continued serving the Lord for the rest of his life. He recently went on to be with the Lord just a few years ago.

Signs, wonders, and miracles became routine, and one day when my dad–Darrel–was asked in class who the family doctor was: my dad responded with, "Doctor Jesus." A realm of the miracle power of Christ was carved out in their family. Everything from words of knowledge, financial multiplication, and significant healing of sickness and disease was a part of growing up in the home.

My grandpa knew religion, and it didn't last, but one encounter with the presence of Jesus not only changed his life forever, but our entire family line.

In Nelson, BC, leaders were hungry for the presence of the Lord. They were tenacious to keep the move of God gospel-centered, and they gave people opportunities to respond to God's presence. What if that meeting had not been hosted?

What if there wasn't a presence-centered community with open doors available when my grandpa needed supernatural divine intervention?

WHAT IS REVIVAL WORTH TO ME? EVERYTHING.

My grandpa was saved in a revival meeting. My dad was saved and called into ministry in a revival meeting. I was saved, baptized in the Holy Spirit, and called into the ministry (three separate occasions). Yes, you guessed it. They were all in revival meetings.

My life was changed because of a supernatural revival dynamic, a realm that was created by radical hunger and empowered and cultivated through intentional leaders.

. . .

RETURN TO YOUR FIRST LOVE

Time without intentionality, can rob us of our first love. I am sure you recognize the phrase "first love" in Revelation 2:4. I have heard this text interpreted like it is referring to our first girlfriend or boyfriend or first marriage. It is not. The term first love in Revelation 2:4 refers to the loved one had at first. The invitation in the text means to go back and remember the intensity, quality, and quantity of love at the very beginning of the relationship.

This is one of the reasons pornography is so destructive for a marriage. It creates simulated experience that involves expectation and preparation. It's secretive, and it creates a sense of thrill and adventure. As the brain processes through the varying emotions that pornography demands, the overall ritual leaves the person drained of ambition and incapable of romantic creativity with their spouse. If the behavior is not addressed, the river of love within the context of marriage will slow until it is nothing more than a stagnant swamp.

Getting back to our first love involves addressing every form of counterfeit intimacy, including eliminating all virtual stimuli allowing us to escape reality, then spending our time on fruit, delaying activity. This is the invitation from the Father for us to prioritize "by His Spirit" over "our own might."

A decision has to be made. Is life going to be a partnership with God, or are we going to try solopreneur kingdom realities without the power of the King? Functioning from first love has to be our motivator. If we have fallen out of love with God and people, if our hearts have become hard and our words harsh, then may we have enough sensitivity to listen to Holy Spirit or the concerned people in our community to acknowledge, confess, and believe that the Lord desires to restore us.

Yes, if we are going to carve out revival realms, then we have to be honest enough to admit that the Lord will never allow His active and manifest presence to be simply an add-on, an upgrade, or a flashy widget to add value to our thing. Revival recentralizes the focus and mission of everything; it places the King and His kingdom in the center of all activity and worship.

THE TENSION IN REVIVAL

There is always tension in a revival dynamic. When people are liberated from all hope, deferred and unshackled from the confines of corporate spirituality, there is a sense of divine restoration that gets everybody wonderfully anxious. When the gifts of the spirit begin to blossom, and the offices of the church begin to unfold, there is an overwhelming sense of such personal significance and the corporate possibility that within the hearts of anyone with a leadership anointing begins to experience the effects of a low-voltage tension.

The tension is the gravity, energy, and the possibility everybody feels. The only way I can describe it is, let's say, that you are at the park with a bunch of friends, and a large gold nugget falls from the sky and hits the ground. Nobody caught it, but everybody saw it. Everybody has equal ownership and responsibility, and everybody is immediately rich. Of course, everybody is excited. Some people are laughing, some people are crying, and some people are passing out. Everybody knows they are now debt-free, and there are things that are possible that previously were not. A few minutes pass before people's giftings start to employ. All of a sudden, the accountants begin counting how many people are in the group while estimating the value of the nugget based on the size, the visionaries begin declaring how the world will be better because of this gold, the teachers start warning people of how excessive wealth can be harmful, the financial advisors begin handing out business cards, and a few people are thinking about how they could manage to steal the gold nugget and have it all to themselves.

This a picture of the tension that exists when God inhabits the realms which we prepared for Him. Things get tense. For this reason, it is crucial that we have values, and corporately, we have values. Values hold us accountable.

In February of 2016, as we began to run with nightly meetings, I released a video to the congregation where I reminded them that community is a core value at SRC and that we are encouraging everyone to attend their home groups still and to prefer their home groups over the revival meetings. Amid the excitement surrounding extended meetings, the people at Seattle Revival Center decided to step into the tension of community and the awakening, and they attended both. Instead of revival killing our group's system, it enhanced and deepened it. Our home groups became revival groups. They grew larger, and SRC grew deeper. We must articulate what we will not compromise before the tension starts. There needs to be an agreed-upon mission, clearly defined values, and rhythms that define a person, family, and organization that will be a part of the wineskin.

I recently captured a podcast with Father John Roddam, the rector at St. Luke's Episcopal church in Seattle. St. Luke's was the church where the charismatic revival broke out in 1969 with Dennis Bennett. Thousands of Catholics were filled with the Holy Spirit and received the gift of tongues. I asked John how revival changed or demolished the traditional liturgical service agenda. John gently informed me that it didn't. The Holy Spirit honored their wineskin and flowed amid their liturgies.

UNGODLY BELIEFS OF THE FALSE REVIVAL MINDSET

A charismatic principality of thought taught that if it's earthly and of the mind, then it is fleshly, worldly, and therefore "bad." This mindset goes back to 1st century gnostic heresy. The ungodly belief (or UGB) that "the visible realm (the body and soul) is bad and only the invisible (the spirit) is good" inspired religious separatism and escapism in the name of Christian holiness.

Mark A. Noll, in his book *The Scandal of Evangelical Mind*, accuses (perhaps accurately) revivalism, and its subsequent theology, as the reason for the abdication of Christian leadership and excellence in the culture. His presupposition argues that if believers praise God with their minds, there will be distinctive intellectual integrity that would begin to demand recognition within the culture. His book argues that believers must see their minds and creation as "good."

When we accuse logic as being the ultimate revival villain, we are hypocritically cursing the biblical government by which we are empowered to steward life and kingdom affairs. It's hypocritical to attack human thought is because this judgment originated from our ability to think. This is similar to the evolutionist who mocks people of faith for their faith when it requires an insane amount of faith to believe that humans evolved from one cute little tadpole whose fairy godmother tapped him with a wand, vanished his tail, and magically transformed him into Hairy the Neanderthal, a gorilla-like mammal who loves tools and chicken wings.

Logic and reason submitted within the context of community and accountability and held within the tension of the word of God and the leading of His voice is not a revival defeater, but an actual core value needed to prepare, steward, and sustain a move of God. What are you seeing, and what are you not seeing? What are the beliefs that exist within your culture that are enabling negative behaviors and undesired results? Is the problem the absence of wine, or is the problem a hidden tear within your wineskin?

GOD FIRST OR PEOPLE FIRST?

A tension I felt in being a pastor is whether our mission should be primarily God-focused or people-focused. As a church, do we seek people, or do we seek Jesus? Now, to the untrained ear, most charismatics would respond, "We seek God first!" So, what does it look like if we seek God first? The obvious answer would include placing a priority on prayer, praise, worship, and preferably worship which is so sincere and hungry that God has no choice. He must come. Meanwhile, new people are not coming. Why? Because they don't know about the church. There's nothing online. The website is out of date. Social media is like a ghost town.

If a family happens to find the church, perhaps through angelic mediation, it takes them ten minutes to figure out how to get into the building because there's inadequate direction. Once the family gets into the building, they sit in their seats and wait for everybody to show up because only new people show up on time. Why? Because they don't know the church culture yet and have not been trained.

Finally, the worship starts. The guitar is out of tune, the sound system sounds muffled, and about thirty minutes into worship, the drummer finally arrives. Running up alongside the chairs, he sits on the drum stool to be part of the last four tunes. After an hour of grueling music that we call worship because it's being performed "for God" and absolutely not for people, the preaching begins. For the next hour, we are lectured through a sequence of peeves, a randomized assortment of text copied and pasted out of the Bible, and an appeal to stop trying to make people happy, "because that is not what we do here at the Keeping It Real Revival Church."

The new family gives genuine thanks to the Lord once they are released from the church service, never to darken the doors of another church again.

Sometimes our pride in presenting "presence-centeredness" can become an excuse to neglect people and the excellence required to truly welcome and disciple people. We would never say this, but sometimes we think we don't have to love people because we are devoting the majority of our bandwidth to loving God. After all, if you are genuinely going after God, can you really be in sin? This is what takes up back to ungodly beliefs and a false revival mindset.

In 1 Kings 18:20-40, we face the famous power struggle between Elijah and the prophets of Baal. Elijah challenged the prophets and their god. He's like, "Let's see what your 'god' can do."

And they took the bull given them, prepared it, and then called upon the name of Baal from morning until noon, saying, "O Baal, answer us!" But there was no voice, and no one answered as they limped around the altar they had made. And at noon, Elijah mocked them, saying, *Cry aloud, for he is a god. Either he is musing, or he is relieving himself, or he is on a journey, or perhaps he is asleep and must be awakened." And they cried aloud and cut themselves after their custom with swords and lances, until the blood gushed out upon them. And as midday passed, they raved on until the time of the offering of the oblation, but there was no voice. No one answered. No one paid attention"* (1 Kings 18:28, 29, ESV).

This is what a lot of modern revivals look like, minus the cutting and bleeding. There is a lot of desperate activity that seems to be a form of veil rending; the only problem is, there is no more veil. Sometimes, in our attempt to "put God first" in our church cultures, we end up creating cultures where corporately we attempt to remove a veil that already removed. If there is no more veil now, then where is God?

Paul gives us a clue in Romans 6. *For if we have been united with him in a death like his, we will certainly also be united with him in a resurrection like his. For we know that our old self was crucified with him so that the body ruled by sin might be done away with, that we should no longer be slaves to sin— because anyone who has died has been set free from sin. Now if we died with Christ, we believe that we will also live with him. For we know that since Christ was raised from the dead, he cannot die again; death no longer has mastery over him. The death he died, he died to sin once for all; but the life he lives, he lives to God* (6:5-10, NIV).

His manifest presence no longer resides in a burning bush or on a holy mountain. He's no longer contained in His studio apartment, a tent where he rarely got to see people. The manifest relational fire glory is now abiding in us! The death he died, he died once for the sin of all so that we can be permanently united, as one, forever.

Andrea and I are married. We are one flesh and are confident in our union. Therefore, when people come to our home, we host our guests and not each other. We are confident in our relationship and covenant; therefore, we don't stress about making each other happy when we are hosting. We partner together to create a lovely experience for our friends and family.

What would it look like to create cultures where we partner with God in confident union to host environments where people could be awakened to their identity and authority in Christ Jesus?

Did Jesus neglect people because his love for His Father was greater than his love for people? Nope. In Luke 19:10, Jesus was like, "Hey, I am here for you!"

RETURN TO THE FATHERS FIRST LOVE

Returning to our first love doesn't just involve falling back in love with God, but also falling back in love with the Father's first love, people. Yes, God loves people!!!

No people, no love. No love, no revival. These words and themes are all intertwined.

When we discuss the wineskin sequence: expectation, preparation, communication, collaboration, celebration, and evaluation, we can clearly see that none of these values means anything outside an appreciation for relationship and covenant. We don't have to get weird with words, but we must be willing to lay down our premature judgments against words like revival, the church, Holy Spirit, community, and people.

Expectation is not hoping Jesus will show up. It is knowing that Jesus already showed up, and now we engage with the hope of Jesus as we partner together to release the reality of his ever-faithful presence dynamic.

Preparation isn't us getting the dinner table ready for Jesus. It's the Father, Son, Spirit, and us setting the table for the prodigal sons that are heading home.

Do you see how this works? When we shift our separation perspective to a union perspective, we no longer see God competing with man; we see the family of God uniting for the revealing of the new humanity, the new and glorious creation in Christ Jesus.

IF WE FAIL

If we try to carve out a realm where, within the context of community, Jesus can be seen and encountered, and we fail, then we are not transfigured into a disqualified remnant of failure. Failure is the best university you will ever attend if you can refuse to define yourself. You have permission to fail. I would challenge you to fail. For so many people, the fear of failure is a curse that renders a life of fruitlessness. I dare you to apply these principles and to participate in a wineskin dynamic for the sake of love.

IF WE SUCCEED

Imagine if Jesus, the living wine, could be served to cities across the world. Can you see a movement where lust, greed, and selfishness would not corrupt the wineskins? Where the sustainability and integrity of the movement were not contingent on the performance of a benevolent and yet inconsistent Pharaoh! Where leaders mutually were submitted to one another! Where the body of Christ was completely connected underneath the headship of Christ! Where the kingdom of God could be identified by their mutual love and honor!

If we succeed, it will not be because we had the right answers; it will be because we asked the right questions. It will not be because we recognized our individualistic potential; it is because we returned to the blueprint of family.

If we succeed, cultural reformation will be an inevitable manifestation that occurs without our cultural manipulation. The love of Christ replaces the fear of man. The awe of God replaces the worship of man, and the world will begin to see, know, and appreciate the reality of heaven on earth.

In Matthew 18:20, Jesus said, *"For where two or three are gathered in my name, there am I among them."* Jesus is saying if you value this heavenly prototype for relationship and partnership, I will manifest myself through your assembly.

It is time to assemble with intentionality and a renewed agenda. To value the values of the kingdom of heaven, we must realize we have been deputized with the authority and ability to execute justice on the earth. It will be hard work. It will be painful. It will be personal. It will require carving out a reality that perhaps contrasts with the present.

Together, we can create contrasting heavenly communities on the earth. If we succeed, all creation will thank us. The silent groaning for our revealing is still deafening. The nations are raging and waiting for this great epiphany to sink in: We are the sons of God.

Now carve!

MEET DARREN!

DARREN STOTT is a Pastor, Author, Podcaster, Radio Host, and Founder of *Supernaturalist Ministries*. Darren was awarded the Dennis Yarnell Inspiration Award for outstanding contribution to the City of Newcastle in 2016 and has been featured in several prominent publications including The Seattle Times, King 5 News, NPR, Charisma Magazine, Renton Reporter, The Religion News Service and Evening Magazine.

Darren began to flex his ministerial muscles at the age of 27 when he became the Lead Pastor at Seattle Revival Center on Easter of 2009. In 2016 his first book was released, Pattern Interrupt: Dismantle Defeat, Overcome Ordinary, and become a Rumbler. Today, he has helped hundreds of thousands with spiritual and practical guidance through pastoring, public speaking, conferences, consulting, and mentoring.

Darren's holds a Bachelor of Arts specializing in Bible & Theology from Global University. By blending his education and many experiences, he has the aptness to help people deconstruct their incorrect framework of God. He engages people in reconstructing a healthy theology and opportunity for divine encounters that lead to personal and spiritual growth. Darren consults with two neighboring cities, and serves on multiple boards for churches, non-profits, and schools.

On May 8th, 2021, Darren Stott was installed as President of the global ministry network now known as Renaissance Coalition, an organization established by John G. Lake in South Africa (International Faith Congress) and then incorporated in Spokane, Washington in 1947 by his daughter and son-in-law, Wilford and Gertrude Reidt. The organization exist to birth Kingdom Realities on the Earth through relationships, gatherings, equipping, and empowerment.

Darren's greatest joy is his lovely wife, Andrea, and four beautiful kids: Abigail, Peter, Sophia, and Victoria.

His call is to catalyze joy in the lives of others.

Connect with Darren at www.darrenstott.com
or on social media @theDarrenStott.

Darren
STOTT

ENDNOTES

1. Ben Patterson, Deepening Your Conversation with God, (Ada, MI, Baker Publishing, 2001) 171.

2. Marsha Stevens, *For Those Tears I Died.*

3. Blumhofer, Edith L. *The Assemblies of God: A Chapter in the Story of American Pentecostalism.* Volume 1. (Springfield, Missouri: Gospel Publishing House, 1989) Page 42-43.

4. International Standard Bible Encyclopedia, Accessed December 19, 2020, https://biblehub.com/topical/e/expectation.htm.

5. Jentezen Franklin, *The Power of Expectation*, Accessed December 19, 2020, https://jentezenfranklin.org/blog/the-power-of-expectation.

6. Watchman Nee, *The Normal Christian Church Life*, Accessed February 4, 2021, https://www.ministrybooks.org/books.cfm?xid=RQZ6OoTL7UMBI.

7. Richard Nordquist, *What is Communication?* Accessed February 4, 2021, https://www.thoughtco.com/what-is-communication-1689877.

8. Accessed February 4, 2021, https://www.theclassroom.com/what-are-the-causes-of-communication-failure-12084449.html.

9. Mekado Murphy, The Adventures of Spielberg, Accessed February 6, 2021, https://carpetbagger.blogs.nytimes.com/2011/12/20/the-adventures-of-spielberg-an-interview/.

10. Accessed February 8, 2021, https://www.goodreads.com/quotes/2646-the-more-you-praise-and-celebrate-your-life-the-more.